Data Analytics: From Foundation to Specialization (2025 Edition)

Azhar ul Haque Sario

Copyright

First Printing, 2025

Azhar.sario@hotmail.co.uk

ORCID: https://orcid.org/0009-0004-8629-830X
LinkedIn: https://www.linkedin.com/in/azharulhaquesario/

Disclaimer: This book is free from AI use. The cover was designed in Microsoft PowerPoint.

This author has no affiliation with the board and it is independently produced under nominative fair use.

Contents

PART I: FOUNDATIONS OF DATA ANALYTICS

The Data Analytics Landscape (2025)

1.1: The Modern Data Analytics Lifecycle and Frameworks

In 2025, data analytics is no longer a niche, back-office function. It has become the central nervous system of an organization. At its core, data analytics is the structured, human-centric practice of examining data. It's not about numbers for the sake of numbers. It's about a formal process of inquiry, a way to ask intelligent questions of our digital world, identify meaningful trends that are often hidden in the noise, and, most importantly, extract actionable insights that drive better decisions. This entire process is guided by a conceptual map, a framework we call the data analytics lifecycle. This lifecycle provides the flow, the series of steps that take raw, chaotic data and transform it into strategic business value.

For decades, the gold standard for this process has been the CRoss-Industry Standard Process for Data Mining (CRISP-DM). This framework is comprehensive, robust, and remains incredibly relevant. It provides a structured, six-phase approach that, when followed, ensures a project doesn't just produce an interesting model, but one that actually solves the problem it set out to address.

The six phases are:

Business Understanding: This is the most critical and most frequently overlooked phase. Before a single line of code is written, the team must define the objective from a business perspective. What problem are we really trying to solve? What is the specific question? What does success look like, and how will we measure it? A failure here guarantees a failure at the end. For example, a vague goal like "improve sales" is useless. A good business understanding is: "We want to increase the average order value of online shoppers by 10% in the next quarter by identifying and promoting high-margin product bundles."

Data Understanding: This phase starts with an initial data collection. Here, the team gets its hands dirty. You explore the data, much like an archaeologist at a new dig site. What data do we have? Is it in a database, or is it a collection of text files? What do the columns mean? Are there obvious errors? This phase is about a first-pass "gut check" to see if the data we have can even possibly answer the question from phase one.

Data Preparation: This is the heavy lifting. In fact, many analysts will tell you this phase consumes 60% to 80% of the entire project. This is where the raw data is cleaned, formatted, and transformed. It involves handling missing values (e.g., should a missing age be filled with the average, or should the row be deleted?), removing duplicate entries, and feature engineering—the creative process of creating new data fields from existing ones. For instance, instead of just having a "purchase_timestamp," you might create new features like "day_of_week" or "time_of_day" to see if patterns exist there.

Modeling: This is the "sexy" part often associated with data science. Here, statistical and machine learning techniques are applied to the prepared data. This could be a simple regression model to predict housing prices or a complex neural network to identify fraud. The key is to select a model that is appropriate for the business problem. A simple, interpretable model is often far better than a complex "black box" one.

Evaluation: The model is built, but is it any good? This phase rigorously tests the model against the business success criteria defined back in phase one. Does the model actually identify good product bundles? How accurate is it? More importantly, where does it fail? Does it perform poorly for a specific customer segment? This is the last stop for quality control before the model impacts the real world.

Deployment: A model sitting in a data scientist's notebook is worthless. Deployment is the process of integrating the model into the existing business operations. This could mean building a new dashboard for the marketing team, creating an automated alert for the fraud department, or plugging the model directly into the e-commerce website to show live recommendations.

The traditional view of CRISP-DM is that it's a "waterfall" process, where you must fully complete one phase before moving to the next. However, the 2025 reality is that data analytics is agile. Modern teams don't wait six months to deliver a single, perfect "big bang" project. They work in "vertical slices." They might take a tiny piece of the problem through all six phases in just two weeks to deliver a small piece of value, get feedback, and then iterate. This agile, iterative workflow is far more responsive to the fast-changing needs of a modern business.

This agility is being supercharged by automation. As of 2025, we are deep in a trend that Gartner predicted: that by 2027, AI-enhanced workflows will reduce manual intervention in data management by 60%. This isn't science fiction. It's happening now. This automation is precisely targeted at that massive 60-80% "Data Preparation" phase. AI-powered tools now automatically scan data for quality issues, suggest cleaning strategies, and even perform complex feature engineering (a process called AutoML), freeing the human analyst to focus on the two phases that require true human intelligence: Business Understanding (asking the right questions) and Evaluation (interpreting the results).

To manage this complex, high-speed, automated flow, a complete modern framework now consists of nine core components. Think of these as the plumbing and architecture of a "data factory." These include ingestion (getting the data in), quality control (the automated checks), governance (rules for who can see what), activation (the pipes to send insights out to tools), and automation (the engine that runs the factory). This architecture ensures that data isn't just a one-time project but a continuous, reliable, and actionable resource.

Updated Application: The "Ask, Prepare, Process..." Model

For new students and professionals, the six-phase CRISP-DM can feel overwhelming. A more intuitive and practical application of the same principles is the simplified, six-step "Ask, Prepare, Process, Analyze, Share, Act" model. This is the mental checklist that an analyst runs through for every single task, whether it's a five-minute query or a five-month project.

This model is designed to take a vague, high-level business problem and break it down into a concrete analytics plan. Let's take the example, "We want to improve customer retention." An analyst can't do anything with that. It's too broad.

Using the framework, they start with "Ask."

Ask: The analyst must go back to the stakeholders and define the specific business problem. They ask clarifying questions: "What do you mean by 'retention'? Are we talking about customers who don't buy a second time, or customers who cancel their subscription?" "How are we measuring it now?" "What is the goal? To reduce churn by 5%?" Through this dialogue, the vague problem becomes a specific, measurable analytics question: "What are the key drivers of subscription cancellation in the first 90 days?"

With a clear question, the analyst moves to the technical work.

Prepare: This is the data gathering stage. Where does the data live? The analyst identifies and pulls data from multiple sources: the subscription database (start/end dates), the customer demographics table (age, location), the app usage logs (how often they log in), and the customer support system (did they file a complaint?).

Process: This maps directly to CRISP-DM's "Data Preparation." The gathered data is a mess. The analyst cleans and standardizes it. They handle missing log-in dates, remove duplicate support tickets, and join all the disparate tables into a single, clean "master" dataset ready for analysis.

Now, the analyst can finally think.

Analyze: This is the hunt for patterns. The analyst applies techniques to find the "why." They might find that customers who don't use a specific app feature in their first week are 50% more likely to cancel. They might see a strong correlation between customers who filed a "billing issue" support ticket and churn.

Share: The insight is useless if it stays in a spreadsheet. The analyst must communicate their findings. This involves creating a compelling data story, often using visualizations (dashboards, charts). The key is to not just share the data, but to share the insight. Don't say: "Churn is 15% for users with billing tickets." Say: "Our billing support process is a primary driver of customer churn, costing us X dollars per month."

Act: This final step closes the loop. The insight is transformed into a strategic decision. The "Share" phase convinced leadership of the problem. The "Act" phase is the solution. For example: "Based on the finding, we recommend creating a proactive outreach program for all customers who file a billing ticket to ensure their issue is resolved and offer a one-time service credit."

Real-Time Case Study 1: "The Bike Share Model"

This case study is a perfect, practical walkthrough of the six-step process. A bike-share company has a key business problem: "How can we convert casual riders into annual members?" Casual riders pay per ride, while members pay an upfront annual fee. The business goal is to create more stable, predictable revenue.

Ask: The analyst defines the problem. The core question is: "What are the behavioral and demographic differences between casual riders and annual members?" The hypothesis is that these two groups use the service in fundamentally different ways.

Prepare: The data is gathered. This includes ride logs (trip duration, start/end station, start/end time, bike ID) and user data (user type: 'casual' or 'member').

Process: The data is cleaned. This is a crucial step. The team removes trips that are less than 60 seconds (likely false starts) and any internal test rides. They handle missing data and ensure the 'user_type' field is consistent.

Analyze: The team applies analytical techniques. They start summarizing and visualizing. The "Aha!" insight emerges:

Finding 1: Annual members' trips are, on average, shorter (e.g., 12 minutes) but far more frequent. They use the bikes for a daily commute.

Finding 2: Casual riders' trips are, on average, longer (e.g., 45 minutes) and far less frequent. They spike on sunny weekends, suggesting tourism or leisure use.

Share: The analyst team communicates these findings. They present a simple, powerful chart showing "Average Trip Duration" and "Rides per Week" for both groups. The story is clear: "We have two different products. Members use us as a utility (like a bus), and casual riders use us as an experience (like a rental car)."

Act: This insight leads to a brilliant strategic decision. The old model was "pay-per-ride" or "pay-for-a-year." This is a huge jump. The data suggests a bridge is needed. The company acts by creating a new pricing model: a "Ride Pack" (e.g., a 3-ride pass for a small discount). This new product is tailored specifically to the casual rider's behavior, encouraging them to ride more often and providing a gentle on-ramp to a full membership.

Real-Time Case Study 2: Retail Customer Analytics (2025)

A major e-commerce retailer is facing intense competition. Their "Business Understanding" phase lands on a clear problem: "Our customer acquisition cost (CAC) is rising, but our customer lifetime value (CLV) is flat. We need to increase CLV by improving personalization."

Ask: How can we use our data to create a truly personalized shopping experience that increases repeat purchases?

Prepare: The data sources are vast and diverse. The team pulls structured data from Point-of-Sale (POS) systems (what you bought, when, which store), website clicks, and loyalty program databases. They also pull unstructured data from product reviews and social media comments.

Process: This is a massive data engineering task. All these sources are cleaned and integrated to create a single, unified "360-degree customer view."

Analyze: With this unified view, the team applies segmentation models. They find several "personas," but one is key: "The High-Potential, One-Time Buyer." This is a customer who spends a lot on their first purchase but never returns. The analysis shows they typically buy a "gateway" product (like a high-end coffee maker) but are never successfully cross-sold the "consumable" (the coffee pods).

Share: The analytics team presents this finding to the marketing department. They show that the current marketing is one-size-fits-all. The "High-Potential" segment is getting generic "20% off" coupons instead of intelligent recommendations.

Act: The company launches a new, data-driven strategy. They activate the insight. Now, when a customer buys the coffee maker, they are automatically placed into a new marketing funnel. Three weeks later, they receive a targeted email (not with a random coupon) but with recommendations for coffee pods that are highly rated by other customers who bought the same machine. This targeted, relevant personalization directly addresses the analytical finding and demonstrably increases repeat purchases and CLV.

This lifecycle, whether CRISP-DM or the "Ask, Act" model, is the foundational skill. It's the "scientific method" for business. The most critical skill in this entire process, as defined by CRISP-DM, is that first phase: Business Understanding. This is the art of Strategic Planning & Problem Formulation. Without it, you are just an order-taker. You are a "code monkey" who can run a query. With it, you are a strategic partner. You are the person who can sit with a confused executive, listen to their vague problem, and use your analytical mind to translate it into a specific, solvable, high-value question. That skill—asking the right question—is more valuable than any technical tool you will ever learn.

1.2: Core Data Structures and Types for Analytics

To be a data analyst, you must first understand your raw material. Data isn't just an abstract concept; it has physical, defined shapes. The way data is organized—its structure—is the most important factor in determining how it can be stored, managed, and, ultimately, analyzed. If you try to analyze data without understanding its underlying structure, it's like trying to build a house without knowing the difference between a wooden beam, a concrete block, and a pane of glass. Each has a different purpose and different properties.

From an analyst's perspective, we classify data into three main structures. This is the first and most important classification you must learn.

1. Structured Data

This is the most traditional and "cleanest" form of data. Structured data adheres to a pre-defined, rigid data model. Think of an Excel spreadsheet or, more formally, a relational database. It is organized into tables with precise rows (records) and columns (attributes).

What it is: Every row in a "Customer" table has the same set of columns: CustomerID, FirstName, LastName, Email. Each column has a defined data type (e.g., CustomerID is a number, FirstName is a string of text, JoinDate is a date).

Where you find it: This is the bedrock of all business operations. Financial transaction logs, e-commerce order tables, patient medical records (the structured parts, like name and date of birth), and inventory systems are all structured data.

How you analyze it: It is straightforward to analyze because it's so organized. The entire language of SQL (Structured Query Language) was invented specifically to "ask questions" of this type of data.

Example: An e-commerce company's "Orders" table is a perfect example. Every single order has an OrderID, a CustomerID, a Timestamp, and a TotalAmount. An analyst can easily use SQL to ask, "What was our total sales revenue for last Tuesday?" by summing the TotalAmount column for records where the Timestamp falls on that day.

2. Unstructured Data

This is the new frontier. Unstructured data is information that has no pre-defined data model or organizational structure. It is the data of human expression. It is estimated that as of 2025, 80-90% of all new data generated by organizations is unstructured.

What it is: Plain text from emails, customer support chats, and social media posts. Video files from security cameras or social media. Audio files from call center recordings. Images and satellite photography. PDF documents and PowerPoint presentations.

Where you find it: Everywhere. It's the text in a product review, the video in a Tesla's camera, the voice of a customer complaining in a support call.

How you analyze it: This data is incredibly rich but "messy" and difficult to analyze with traditional tools. You can't use SQL to "query" a video. Analyzing it requires advanced techniques, typically from the world of AI and machine learning. You use Natural Language Processing (NLP) to understand the sentiment of a customer email or Computer Vision to identify a defective product on an assembly line from a video feed.

Example: A company wants to understand why customers are giving its new product bad reviews. The "star rating" (1-5 stars) is structured data. But the reason is locked inside the unstructured text of the review: "The battery life is terrible and it feels cheap." An analyst must use NLP models to scan thousands of reviews and extract these common themes to provide actionable feedback to the product team.

3. Semi-Structured Data

This is the flexible middle ground between the two extremes. Semi-structured data does not fit into the rigid rows and columns of a relational database, but it does contain tags or markers to separate semantic elements and create hierarchies.

What it is: The two most common forms are JSON (JavaScript Object Notation) and XML (eXtensible Markup Language). These formats use key-value pairs and tags to create a "tree-like" structure.

Where you find it: This is the language of the modern internet. When you load a webpage, the server often sends data to your browser as a JSON object. Web APIs, which allow different applications to talk to each other, almost exclusively use JSON. System logs are often semi-structured.

How you analyze it: It is more flexible than structured data (you can easily add new fields without breaking the whole table) but far easier to parse and query than unstructured data. Many modern databases are designed to store and query JSON data directly.

Example: A user profile on a website might be stored as a JSON object. It has clear tags, but it's flexible.
JSON

```
{
  "userID": 12345,
  "username": "data_analyst_pro",
  "joined_date": "2024-10-01",
```

```
  "interests": [
    "data visualization",
    "python",
    "machine learning"
  ],
  "location": {
    "city": "New York",
    "country": "USA"
  }
}
```

You can see the hierarchy. The interests key points to a list of items. The location key points to another object with its own keys. This flexibility is extremely powerful.

Updated Application: Matching Problems to Structures

Beyond these high-level classifications, data is organized in specific programmatic data structures that a computer understands. An analyst doesn't need to be an expert programmer, but they do need to understand why these structures matter for analysis.

Arrays (or Lists): This is the simplest structure, an ordered list of items. Its primary analytical use is for time-series data. Financial stock data is a perfect example. The order is critical. The price from Monday must come before the price from Tuesday. Storing this in an Array or list (e.g., [150.10, 152.05, 151.80]) maintains this crucial linear order.

Hash Tables (or Dictionaries): This is one of the most powerful structures for analysis. It stores data in key-value pairs. This allows for instantaneous lookups. If you have a massive table of 100 million customers, finding a specific CustomerID can be slow. But if you store it as a hash table (where the key is the CustomerID and the value is the customer's name), you can retrieve any customer's data instantly, no matter how large the dataset.

Graphs: This structure is designed to model relationships. A graph consists of nodes (entities) and edges (the relationships between them). As the prompt notes, a social network is the classic example: you are a node, your friend is a node, and the "friendship" is the edge. But the applications go far deeper.

Real-Time Case Study 1: Graph Analytics for Fraud Detection

Let's look at a powerful, real-world application of a graph data structure. A bank wants to detect a "fraud ring"—a group of criminals opening fake accounts to launder money.

In a Structured (Relational) Model: The bank has a "Customer" table and an "Account" table. To find a fraud ring, an analyst would have to write incredibly complex SQL queries to join tables on shared IP_Address, then join again on shared PhoneNumber, then join again on shared Physical_Address. This is extremely slow and often misses complex patterns.

In a Graph Model: The analyst models the data differently.

Customer, PhoneNumber, IP_Address, and Account are all Nodes.

"HAS_PHONE," "LOGGED_IN_FROM," and "OWNS_ACCOUNT" are Edges.

Now, the analyst can ask powerful questions. "Show me all nodes that share more than one connection." Instantly, the graph reveals a pattern that was invisible before: two different customers (Node A and Node B) are linked to the same PhoneNumber (Node C) and also made transactions from the same IP_Address (Node D). This "connected component" is a massive red flag for a fraud ring.

Companies like Neo4j specialize in this. A real-world case study with Banking Circle found that by using graph data science, they were able to identify complex money laundering networks that their traditional systems missed. They halved the number of alerts escalated for manual review, freeing up their human investigators to focus on real crime instead of false positives. This is a perfect example of how choosing the correct data structure is a critical analytical skill.

Real-Time Case Study 2: "Tesla's Autopilot Data"

This is the ultimate example of a hybrid-data problem, where all three data structures (structured, unstructured, and semi-structured) must work together to solve a single, complex problem.

Tesla's goal is to train an AI that can drive a car. To do this, it must collect and analyze data from its global fleet of vehicles. This data is a complex fusion:

Structured Data: This is the high-frequency sensor data. It's a constant stream of numbers in a rigid format: Timestamp, Speed, Acceleration, Steering_Wheel_Angle, Temperature, GPS_Coordinates. This data is clean, fast, and perfect for understanding the car's physical state.

Unstructured Data: This is the richest and most complex data: the raw video feeds from the car's eight onboard cameras. This is what the car "sees." It's just a stream of pixels. This data is used to train the computer vision models to "see" and "classify" the world (e.g., "that's a 'stop sign'," "that's a 'pedestrian'," "that's a 'truck'").

Semi-Structured Data: This is the glue that provides context. The car's internal systems generate constant system logs and error messages, often in a JSON format. For example: {"event": "AUTOPILOT_DISENGAGEMENT", "timestamp": "...", "reason": "USER_OVERRIDE"}.

The magic of Tesla's system is data fusion. The structured data provides context for the unstructured data. When the AI model makes a mistake (e.g., it suddenly slams on the brakes), the engineers can investigate. They pull the unstructured video for that exact moment and see what the car saw (e.g., a plastic bag blowing across the road). Then, they look at the structured data (the car's speed and braking) and the semi-structured logs (which system made the decision?). This proprietary dataset, combining all three types, is what allows them to find these "edge cases" and constantly retrain their AI models to navigate complex, real-world traffic scenarios.

This leads to the core job skill: Data Acumen & Foundational Computer Science. Data acumen is the intuition an analyst develops. It's the ability to hear a business problem and immediately start thinking about the underlying data. "You want to analyze customer churn? Okay, I'll need the structured subscription table. I'll also want to see the unstructured support emails. And I'll bet the app's semi-structured JSON logs will tell me what features they're using." This foundational understanding of how data is stored, organized, and retrieved is the prerequisite for all advanced analysis. It's the bridge between the business world and the technical world.

1.3: The 2025 Analytics Ecosystem: Roles and Responsibilities

The field of "data" is not one single job. It's a complex, collaborative ecosystem of roles, each with a distinct focus, skillset, and set of responsibilities. As the industry has matured, these roles have become more specialized. To build a career in data, the first step is to understand the map—to know who does what and why.

Think of a data project as a sophisticated oil exploration and refinement operation. You need a team.

The Data Analyst is the geologist. They are on the ground, taking samples, and drawing the maps. They use historical data to answer, "Where did we find oil?" (What happened?) and "Why do we think it's concentrated in this area?" (Why?).

The Data Scientist is the physicist and petroleum engineer. They use the geologist's maps to build complex predictive models. They answer, "If we drill here, what are the chances we hit a major deposit, and how much will we get?" (What will happen?) and "What is the optimal extraction strategy to get the most oil out for the least cost?" (What is the best-case scenario?).

The Machine Learning Engineer is the industrial engineer and rig operator. They take the scientist's complex extraction blueprint and build the multi-million dollar production rig. They are responsible for making the model work safely, efficiently, and at a massive scale, 24/7, without breaking.

In 2025, these three primary roles define the core of the data ecosystem.

The Data Analyst: The "What" and "Why"

The Data Analyst is the primary storyteller and the most direct link between raw data and business decision-makers. Their focus is on the past and the present. They are experts at cleaning, querying, and visualizing data to generate insights and reports.

Core Question: "What happened last quarter, and why did it happen?"

Day-to-Day: An analyst lives inside tools like SQL, Excel, and business intelligence (BI) platforms like Tableau and Power BI. Their day consists of writing SQL queries to pull data from a database, cleaning and analyzing that data (often in Excel or a Python notebook), and building interactive dashboards that allow executives to see what's happening.

Example: A marketing manager asks, "How did our holiday email campaign perform?" The Data Analyst will query the database, segment customers by who opened the email and who didn't, and present a dashboard showing that the campaign led to a 15% increase in sales for that cohort, but that the "20% off" coupon was twice as effective as the "Free Shipping" offer.

The Data Scientist: The "What If"

The Data Scientist is a builder of predictive models. Their focus is on the future. They use a deeper toolkit of statistics and machine learning to forecast and optimize. They are less concerned with reporting on what happened and more concerned with building a system that can predict what will happen.

Core Question: "Which of our customers are most likely to churn next month?"

Day-to-Day: A data scientist lives in programming languages like Python or R, using advanced libraries (like Scikit-learn or TensorFlow). They spend their time training, testing, and validating statistical models. They are often more research-oriented and have a stronger background in mathematics and statistics.

Example: Following the analyst's report, the Data Scientist takes all the data from past campaigns and builds a machine learning model. This model "learns" the patterns of customers who respond best to coupons. The output of their work is a new tool that can "score" every customer from 1-100 on their likelihood to respond to a "20% off" offer, allowing the company to target only the right customers and save millions.

The Machine Learning Engineer: The "How-to-at-Scale"

The Machine Learning Engineer (MLE) is the fastest-growing and, in 2025, one of the most critical roles. This is a highly specialized software engineering role that focuses on one thing: productionalization. It's not enough for a data scientist's model to work on their laptop. The MLE figures out how to make it work for 10 million users in real-time.

Core Question: "How do we deploy this churn model so it runs every night, scales to our entire user base, and doesn't crash our servers?"

Day-to-Day: The MLE lives in a world of cloud platforms (AWS, Google Cloud), containerization tools (Docker, Kubernetes), and MLOps (Machine Learning Operations) pipelines. They write the "production" code—the high-performance, fault-tolerant code—that integrates the model into a live application. They are also responsible for A/B testing, monitoring the model for "drift" (when its predictions get worse over time), and managing the entire model lifecycle.

Example: The MLE takes the Data Scientist's model and builds an API (Application Programming Interface) around it. They work with the web development team to "call" this API. Now, when a customer with a high churn score logs into the website, the MLE's system instantly triggers a pop-up with a special retention offer. They are the ones who turn the "prediction" into an automated action.

Updated Application: Mapping Your Career Path

Understanding these roles allows you to map a practical career. The most common pathway is to start as a Data Analyst. This role provides the best possible foundation, forcing you to learn the business, master SQL, and develop communication skills. From there, the paths diverge.

The Upskill Path (Analyst -> Data Scientist): An analyst who loves the statistical and modeling parts of their job can upskill to become a Data Scientist. This involves a deep dive into Python/R, advanced statistics, and machine learning principles. They trade their dashboard-building time for model-building time.

The Management Path (Analyst -> Analytics Manager): An analyst who excels at communication, strategy, and stakeholder management can move into leadership. An Analytics Manager or, eventually, a Chief Data Officer (CDO), spends less time writing queries and more time managing a team, defining the company's data strategy, and ensuring the analytics team is solving the right business problems.

The "T-Shaped" Professional: In 2025, the most valuable professionals are "T-shaped." This means they have deep expertise in one area (the vertical bar of the "T") but broad, functional knowledge of the other areas (the horizontal bar). A T-shaped analyst not only masters SQL and Tableau, but also understands the basics of machine learning (so they can work with scientists) and the fundamentals of data engineering (so they know where their data comes from).

Real-Time Case Study 1: "The 2025 Job Market Analysis"

A 2024-2025 job market analysis (like those published by data-driven platforms) reveals a critical, nuanced shift in the industry, which provides a data-driven justification for the roles as we've defined them.

Role	Job Postings Volume	Year-over-Year Growth	Median Salary (Mid-Level)
Data Analyst	~45,230	+12%	~$95,000
Machine Learning Engineer	~19,780	+34% (Explosive)	~$165,000
Data Scientist	~28,950	-8% (Contracting)	~$130,000

This data tells a fascinating story:

Data Analyst roles are the bedrock. They dominate in sheer volume and are still growing healthily. Every company needs people who can understand and visualize data.

Machine Learning Engineer roles are exploding. The +34% growth is a direct result of AI integration. Companies have spent the last five years building models; they are now desperately hiring engineers who can deploy them.

The high salary reflects the high demand and specialized software engineering skillset.

Data Scientist roles are contracting. This is the most misunderstood trend. It does not mean data science is "dying." It means the "generalist" Data Scientist title from 2018 is being unbundled. The "reporting" part of the job is being absorbed by high-skilled Data Analysts. The "deployment" part of the job is being taken over by ML Engineers. The remaining "Data Scientist" roles are becoming more specialized (e.g., "NLP Scientist," "Computer Vision Scientist," "Causal Inference Scientist"), often requiring a Ph.D. or deep domain expertise. This contraction is a sign of maturity, not decline.

Real-Time Case Study 2: Spotify's "Squad" Model

How do these roles work together in a real company? Spotify provides a world-class example with its famous "Spotify Model." They organize work not by departments, but by autonomous "Squads."

A Squad is a small, cross-functional, self-organizing team with a specific mission (e.g., "Improve the 'Discover Weekly' playlist"). A single squad might include a Product Owner, several Software Engineers, and one Data Analyst.

The Data Analyst on this squad is embedded. They aren't in a separate "analytics department." They sit with the team, participating in every meeting. Their job is to run all the A/B tests for new features, analyze user engagement, and provide the data that guides the squad's next move.

Chapters and Guilds: Spotify then links these roles horizontally. The Data Analyst in the "Discover Weekly" squad also belongs to the "Data Analytics Chapter." This chapter is made up of all the data analysts from all the different squads. They meet regularly to share best practices, discuss new tools (like a new Tableau feature), and maintain their "T-shaped" skills.

This model shows the 2025 ideal: the analyst is not a back-office report-puller. They are a strategic, embedded partner, supported by a "chapter" of their peers, working directly on the front lines of product development.

This brings us to the final job skill: Career Strategy & Industry Awareness. You cannot plan your career without this map. Understanding this ecosystem is a skill in itself. It allows you to look at the job market with data (as in the 2025 analysis) and align your personal learning goals with high-demand, high-growth roles. It empowers you to ask: Am I a storyteller (Analyst)? A researcher (Scientist)? Or a builder (Engineer)? Answering that question is the first step to building a durable, long-term career.

1.4: Introduction to AI and Generative AI in Data Analytics

For the data analyst in 2025, Artificial Intelligence (AI) is not a separate, competing field. It is not a far-off threat. It is a foundational, ever-present accelerator. It is a force multiplier for every single step of the analytics lifecycle. If the data analyst is a skilled artisan, AI is a new suite of power tools. An artisan with power tools can build faster, more precisely, and at a greater scale than one with only hand tools.

Within this broad category of AI, the most transformative technology for analytics today is Generative AI (GenAI). This is a specific subset of AI that leverages massive machine learning models (like Large Language Models, or LLMs) to generate new content rather than just make predictions. This "new content" can be human-like text, audio, images, and, most importantly for us, code.

The application of GenAI in analytics is not about replacing the analyst. It's about augmenting them. It involves automating the most routine, time-consuming tasks, generating data-driven insights on command, and radically speeding up the technical work of data cleaning and analysis.

Updated Application: AI as an Accelerator in the 6-Step Lifecycle

The best way to understand AI's impact is to inject it into the "Ask, Prepare, Process, Analyze, Share, Act" model we discussed. In 2025, an AI-literate analyst uses these tools at every stage.

Ask (AI-Assisted Brainstorming):

Without AI: An analyst manually brainstorms reasons for a problem (e.g., "customer churn is up").

With AI: The analyst opens a GenAI chat interface and prompts it: "Act as a senior retail data analyst. Give me 10 distinct, testable hypotheses for why our e-commerce subscription churn has increased 15% in the last quarter." The AI will instantly generate a list (e.g., "1. A recent price increase. 2. A new competitor's marketing campaign. 3. A bug in the checkout process. 4. Poor performance of our new delivery partner..."). This jump-starts the entire analytical process.

Prepare (AI-Assisted Data Discovery):

Without AI: The analyst manually hunts through data catalogs or asks colleagues, "Where can I find data on delivery partner performance?"

With AI: Modern data platforms have AI-powered data discovery. The analyst can just ask the system, "Find me all datasets related to 'delivery' and 'customer complaints'." The AI suggests the most relevant tables to join.

Process (AI-Assisted Cleaning and Coding):

Without AI: The analyst spends 80% of their time here, writing tedious code (in SQL or Python) to clean data. They might spend an hour trying to remember the complex syntax for a "window function" in SQL.

With AI: This is the biggest accelerator. The analyst uses a GenAI tool (like SQLAI.ai or GitHub Copilot) and writes a natural language prompt: "Write a SQL query that joins the users table and the orders table. For each user, find their total number of orders and their second order date. Only include users from 'New York'." The AI generates the complex, error-free SQL in seconds. This radically lowers the barrier to entry for complex analysis and makes every analyst dramatically more productive.

Analyze (AI-Assisted Insight Generation):

Without AI: The analyst manually "slices and dices" the data, looking for correlations.

With AI: Modern BI tools (like Tableau or Power BI) have AI features built-in. An analyst can upload a dataset, and the tool will automatically run statistical tests and surface "interesting" findings, like "Sales in the 'East' region have the strongest correlation with 'Marketing Spend'."

Share (AI-Assisted Storytelling):

Without AI: The analyst stares at a blank screen, trying to find the right words to summarize their complex findings for an executive.

With AI: The analyst feeds their key findings (the "what") into a GenAI and prompts it: "Write a 3-paragraph executive summary for a marketing VP. Explain that our analysis found that customer churn is primarily driven by poor delivery experiences. Be professional and persuasive." The AI generates a near-perfect draft for the analyst to edit.

Act (AI-Assisted Simulation):

Without AI: The analyst presents their recommendation ("We should switch delivery partners"), but the executives ask, "What's the financial impact?"

With AI: The analyst can use AI-powered simulation models to answer, "Based on the data, switching to a partner with a 99% on-time rate is projected to reduce churn by 3% and increase lifetime value by $1.2 million over the next year."

Real-Time Case Study 1: "Uber's Internal AI Agents"

This case study demonstrates how a data-driven company, Uber, is using custom AI tools not for its customers, but to make its own employees more effective. This is a perfect example of AI augmentation.

Uber launched internal "Business AIgents" to help its customer service representatives. When a user (a driver or rider) starts a chat, the service rep often has to toggle between 10 different screens to understand the context: What was their last trip? What was their complaint last month? What is their current rating?

The Solution: The new AIgent automatically scans all of these data sources in real-time.

The Result: When the support rep opens the chat, the AI agent has already placed a summary in their window: "This is Jane, a 5-star rider. Her last trip ended 10 minutes ago. She is likely contacting you because her driver took a long route, and she was overcharged by $5.30. Her last support ticket two months ago was also about a billing issue."

This AI tool doesn't replace the human. It empowers them. It surfaces context and summarizes complex interactions instantly. This frees the human representative to skip the "data-hunting" phase and focus entirely on the high-value, human-centric tasks of empathy and problem-solving.

Real-Time Case Study 2: GenAI in Logistics and Retail

The use of GenAI as an accelerator is exploding across industries. A Google Cloud report highlights several real-world examples:

Volkswagen: The company is integrating GenAI into its myVW app. A user can now ask the car's manual questions in natural language, like "How do I change a flat tire?" This turns a static, unstructured PDF (the manual) into an interactive, conversational data source.

Domina (Logistics): This Colombian logistics company, which handles over 20 million shipments a year, uses AI to predict package returns (a classic analytics problem) and automate delivery validation. This has led to a 15% increase in delivery effectiveness and eliminated the time spent on manual report generation. The AI does the "Process" and "Analyze" steps automatically.

TruckHouse (Manufacturing): This small company uses Gemini in Google Sheets to speed up inventory tracking. This is a perfect example of AI at the analyst's level. Instead of writing complex spreadsheet formulas, an inventory manager can just ask the sheet, "What is our current stock level for 'Part A', and when do we need to reorder based on last month's sales?"

Job Skill Enhancement: AI Literacy

This new landscape creates a new, non-negotiable baseline requirement for every data role in 2025: AI Literacy.

This does not mean every analyst needs to know how to build a large language model (that's the ML Engineer's job). It means they must know how to use one safely, effectively, and ethically. The World Economic Forum and other thought leaders have defined AI literacy as having four key components:

Problem-Solving: Knowing when and how to use an AI tool to accelerate your workflow.

Innovation: Using GenAI to brainstorm new ideas and analytical approaches you might not have thought of.

Collaboration: Understanding the AI's capabilities so you can work effectively with both the AI and the technical teams (like ML Engineers) who build with it.

AI Safety & Ethics: This is the most important. An AI-literate analyst knows the limitations. They know that GenAI can "hallucinate" (make up confident-sounding, but false, information). They know to never trust a GenAI's output without verifying it themselves. They would never paste sensitive company data (like customer PII) into a public AI tool.

This skill is directly linked to job security. A 2025 PwC survey revealed that 73% of workers at large organizations are confident that AI skills will enhance their job security. A further 92% of employees who use GenAI daily report higher levels of productivity. The message is clear, and it's a quote you'll hear often:

"AI is not going to take your job. A person using AI is going to take your job."

In 2025, AI literacy is the new baseline. It is the evolution of data literacy. It provides the foundational skills that are now a baseline requirement for almost all data analyst roles, allowing you to be not just a data analyst, but an AI-augmented, high-productivity, high-impact strategic partner.

Statistical and Probabilistic Foundations for Analytics

Subtopic 2.1: Descriptive Statistics and Data Distributions

Think of any dataset you first receive as a crowded, chaotic room full of people. If you're asked, "What's this party like?" you wouldn't start by interviewing every single person. You'd probably stand at the door for a moment and observe. You'd get a feel for the room. What's the general age? What's the vibe—is it loud, quiet, or is there a loud group in one corner and a quiet one in another?

This "feel for the room" is precisely what descriptive statistics provide. It's the very first handshake you have with your data, and it's your primary tool for turning a massive, unreadable spreadsheet into a concise, meaningful story. It's the foundation of all exploratory data analysis (EDA). Without this step, you risk building complex, sophisticated models on a foundation of sand.

We do this by summarizing the data in two main ways: finding the "center" and understanding the "spread."

Finding the "Center": Measures of Central Tendency

This is about finding the "typical" data point. But "typical" can mean a few different things, and the difference is crucial.

The Mean (Average): This is the one we all learned in school. Add everything up, divide by how many there are. The mean is democratic; every single data point gets a vote. But this is also its greatest weakness. If you have one massive outlier (like a CEO's salary in a dataset of employee salaries), it will pull the mean significantly in its direction. A company might proudly report an "average salary" of $150,000, but that single $2 million CEO salary could be hiding the fact that 90% of the staff makes $45,000.

The Median (Midpoint): This is the "person in the middle." If you line up all your data points from smallest to largest, the median is the one standing exactly in the middle (or the average of the two middle ones). The median is robust to outliers. It doesn't care about that $2 million salary. It just looks at the line and finds the middle, which might be $48,000. This is often a much more honest representation of the "typical" value, especially in skewed data like income or housing prices.

The Mode (Most Frequent): This is the most common value in the dataset. In our salary example, the mode might be $42,000, representing the most common entry-level salary. The mode is especially useful for categorical data (e.g., "What's the most-sold t-shirt color?").

Understanding the "Spread": Measures of Data Dispersion

Knowing the "center" is only half the story. Two cities can have the same mean annual temperature of 15°C (59°F), but one might be San Francisco (where the temperature is always around 15°C) and the other could be St. Louis (with frigid winters and blazing-hot summers). The experience of living in those cities is totally different. That's dispersion.

Range: The simplest measure. Just the highest value minus the lowest value. It's useful but, like the mean, can be very misleading if you have just one or two extreme outliers.

Variance and Standard Deviation: These are the most important measures of spread. They are essentially the average distance of any data point from the mean. A low standard deviation means all the data points are clustered tightly around the mean (like San Francisco's weather). A high standard deviation means the data is spread all over the place (like St. Louis's weather). In finance, standard deviation is the classic measure of risk or volatility. A stock with a high standard deviation is unpredictable; one with a low one is stable.

The Shape of Data: Key Distributions

Finally, we look at the shape of the data, which often follows predictable patterns.

Normal Distribution: The classic "bell curve."

Shutterstock

Most data points are near the mean, and they get rarer as you move further away. Height, test scores, and manufacturing errors often follow this pattern. It's the "default" assumption in many statistical tests.

Binomial Distribution: This is for data with only two possible outcomes (binary). Think of flipping a coin 100 times. You want to know the probability of getting 60 heads. A/B testing (click vs. no-click), conversion rates (convert vs. no-convert), and pass/fail quality checks all use this.

Poisson Distribution: This distribution is for counting. It models the probability of a certain number of events happening in a fixed interval of time or space. How many customers arrive at a bank in an hour? How many typos are on a page? How many calls will a support center receive at 3:00 PM? If you can model this, you can staff for it.

Real-Time Application: The "J-Shaped" Review

Let's look at that e-commerce product rating case. The mode (most frequent rating) is 5.0 stars. This is fantastic! But the mean (average) is only 4.1 stars. This is the analyst's moment. A simple report of "4.1 stars" is lazy. The real insight comes from the tension between the mode and the mean.

This tells us the distribution is not a nice, symmetrical bell curve. It's "skewed." It's likely a "J-shape," with a huge bar at 5 stars, a much smaller bar at 1 star, and very few 2, 3, and 4-star reviews. This isn't an "average" product; it's a polarizing one. You have a passionate, loyal fanbase (the 5-star crowd) and a small but vocal group of critics (the 1-star crowd).

The business strategy here is not to try and "improve the mean." It's to act on the polarization. The strategy for the 5-star group is about mobilization: get them to write text reviews, refer friends, and join a loyalty program. The strategy for the 1-star group is about damage control and feedback: use their (likely very detailed) reviews to find product flaws, fix bugs, or clarify misleading marketing copy. This is how descriptive statistics, when interpreted thoughtfully, drive high-level business strategy.

🔬 Subtopic 2.2: Inferential Statistics: Hypothesis Testing and Confidence Intervals

Descriptive statistics tell us what happened in the data we have. But we almost never have all the data. We don't have time to survey every customer, test every product, or track every user. We have a sample—a small snapshot of the whole picture.

The big, multi-million-dollar question is: Can we use this small sample to make a reliable decision about the entire population? This is the core of inferential statistics. It's the science of making educated, data-driven leaps of faith. It's how we move from "reporting" to "deciding."

The primary tool for this is Statistical Hypothesis Testing, which is best understood as a "data courtroom." You have a claim you want to test, and you need to see if your evidence (your sample data) is strong enough to "convict" the default assumption.

The Courtroom Drama of Hypothesis Testing

Here are the key players in our trial:

The Null Hypothesis (H0): This is the "default assumption," the status quo. In the courtroom, it's "innocent until proven guilty." In business, it's "there is no change," "this has no effect," or "the new version is the same as the old." For example, H0: "The new website button color does not increase conversions."

The Alternative Hypothesis (H1): This is the prosecutor's claim, the new idea you're testing. H1: "The new website button color does increase conversions."

The Evidence (Your Sample): You run your test and collect data. You find that the new button (Variation B) had a 2.59% conversion rate, while the old one (Control A) had 2.20%. This looks like a win. But... is it a real win, or did Variation B just get lucky? Could this difference have happened by random chance?

The Standard of Proof (Significance Level, a): Before the trial, you must set your "standard of proof." This is the threshold for "beyond a reasonable doubt." In statistics, this is called the Significance Level, or alpha (a). It's almost always set to 0.05 (or 5%). This means you are only willing to accept a 5% risk of being wrong (a "false positive").

The Verdict (The p-value): This is the most misunderstood concept in all of statistics. The p-value is not the probability that your alternative hypothesis is true.

The p-value is the probability of seeing your evidence (or even stronger evidence) if the null hypothesis were true.

Let's re-read that. In our A/B test, a p-value of, say, 0.002 means: "If the new button color truly had no effect (i.e., H0 is true), the probability of us seeing a lift this big or bigger purely by random chance is only 0.2%."

That's a very low probability! It's so low that it's unlikely our null hypothesis is true. Our observed data is highly improbable under the "no effect" assumption.

So, we make our decision:

If p-value $\leqslant \alpha$ ($0.002 \leqslant 0.05$): We reject the Null Hypothesis. The evidence is "beyond a reasonable doubt." We declare the finding "statistically significant" and conclude that the new button is better.

If p-value > a (e.g., p = 0.25 > 0.05): We fail to reject the Null Hypothesis. This doesn't mean the null is true! It just means our evidence wasn't strong enough to convict. We did not prove our case.

The Risks of Getting it Wrong: Type I & II Errors

In this process, we can make two critical mistakes:

Type I Error (False Positive): We reject the null hypothesis, but it was actually true. (We convict an innocent person). This is our A/B test getting a p-value of 0.03 by pure luck, and us launching a "better" button that is, in reality, no different. We waste time and resources implementing a change that does nothing. Our alpha of 0.05 directly controls our risk of this error.

Type II Error (False Negative): We fail to reject the null hypothesis, but it was actually false. (A guilty person walks free). This is our new button actually being better, but our test not having enough power (e.g., too small a sample size) to detect the difference. We miss a major business opportunity.

A More Human Answer: Confidence Intervals

P-values are a "yes/no" decision. But business leaders prefer ranges. This is where Confidence Intervals (CI) come in. A CI gives you a range of plausible values for the true population parameter.

Instead of just saying "the new button is better," a 95% CI provides a much richer answer:

"We are 95% confident that the true lift in conversion from the new button is between +8.1% and +27.2%."

This is incredibly useful. First, note that "0%" is not in this interval. This confirms our hypothesis test: since zero (no effect) is not a plausible value, we can reject the null. Second, it gives the business a best-case and worst-case scenario for the magnitude of the win. It sets realistic expectations. This skill, moving from "reporting data" (descriptive) to "validating decisions" (inferential), is the single biggest leap an analyst can make in their career.

📊 Subtopic 2.3: Correlation and Linear Regression Models

Once we've described our data (Subtopic 2.1) and confirmed our findings are real (Subtopic 2.2), we move to the next logical question: "How are things related?" This is the jump from observing one variable at a time (univariate) to understanding how two variables move together (bivariate).

This is the gateway to predictive modeling. It's the ability to say, "If this changes, we expect that to change by this much." This is the foundation for forecasting, budgeting, and strategic planning.

The First Look: Correlation Analysis

The first step is measuring the relationship between two continuous variables. The most common tool for this is the Pearson correlation coefficient (r).

This r is a single, elegant number that tells you two things about the relationship:

Direction (The Sign: + or -):

A positive (+) r means as one variable goes up, the other tends to go up (e.g., square footage of a house and its price).

A negative (-) r means as one variable goes up, the other tends to go down (e.g., number of hours spent practicing a video game and the number of mistakes made).

Strength (The Number: 0 to 1):

An r close to 1 (or -1) is a strong correlation. The dots on a scatterplot form a tight, clean line.

Shutterstock

* An r close to **0** is a *weak* or *no* correlation. The dots are just a random cloud; there's no discernible pattern.

This is a powerful first diagnostic. But it comes with the most important warning in all of statistics, a phrase that should be tattooed on the arm of every analyst:

Correlation does not imply causation.

Just because two things move together does not mean one causes the other. The classic example is that ice cream sales are highly correlated with drowning incidents. Does ice cream cause drowning? No. A third, "lurking" variable—hot weather—causes both. People buy more ice cream when it's hot, and people swim more (and thus, tragically, drown more) when it's hot.

An analyst who runs to their boss and says, "We must ban ice cream to save lives!" is making a catastrophic error. An analyst who says, "Ice cream sales and drownings are both peaking; it must be summer. Let's ensure we have extra lifeguards staffed on hot days," is doing the job correctly. This is where domain knowledge and human experience are irreplaceable.

From "What?" to "So What?": Simple Linear Regression

Correlation is good for describing a relationship. Linear Regression is how we use it to predict. It's the act of drawing the "best fit line" (technically, the "Ordinary Least Squares" line) through that scatterplot of data.

You're taking that simple 8th-grade formula, y=mx+b, and turning it into a powerful predictive engine:

y is the Dependent Variable: The thing you want to predict (e.g., "Total Monthly Sales").

x is the Independent Variable: The thing you're using to make the prediction (e.g., "Monthly Ad Spend").

b is the Intercept: The baseline. This is the value of y if x were 0. In our case: "What would our sales be if we spent $0 on ads?" This is your baseline from brand equity, foot traffic, etc.

m is the Slope: This is the magic number. This is the coefficient. It tells you, "For every one-unit increase in x, what is the expected increase (or decrease) in y?"

Real-Time Case Study: "Predicting Sales from Ad Spend"

Let's run this model. We feed our past 36 months of data (Ad Spend, Sales) into Python or Excel. The model runs and gives us our answer:

Sales = (1.75 * Ad_Spend) + 35,000

What does this mean?

Intercept (b = 35,000): If we spend $0 on ads, our model predicts we will still make $35,000 in monthly sales. That's our baseline.

Slope (m = 1.75): This is the gold. This is our Return on Ad Spend (ROAS). It means that for every $1.00 we spend on ads, we can expect to get $1.75 back in sales.

This is no longer just "reporting." This is strategy. A manager can now go to the finance department and say, "I need an extra $100,000 for my ad budget. Our model shows a clear, positive ROAS of 1.75. This isn't spending; it's an investment with a predictable return."

How Good is Our "Crystal Ball"? Model Evaluation (R2)

One final step: How good is our model? How reliable is this prediction? For that, we use the R-squared (R2), or the coefficient of determination.

This is a number from 0% to 100% that tells you "how much of the variation (the wiggles) in the dependent variable (y) is explained by the independent variable (x)."

An R2 of 85% would be amazing. It means 85% of the reason our sales go up and down each month is explained by our ad spend. The other 15% is just "noise" (competitor actions, a new product, a holiday, weather—everything else).

An R2 of 10% is terrible. It means ad spend has almost nothing to do with sales. Our model is useless for prediction, and the 1.75 ROAS is probably not a reliable number.

This skill is the true gateway from analyst to data scientist. You are no longer just looking at data; you are modeling it to predict the future.

🧠 Subtopic 2.4: Mathematical Foundations: Applied Linear Algebra

If descriptive statistics, hypothesis testing, and regression are the tools you see in the data scientist's workshop, then linear algebra is the electricity powering them all. You don't necessarily see it, but nothing works without it.

For many, the word "matrix" or "vector" brings back abstract, dry memories from a college math class. But in data analytics, these concepts are incredibly tangible, practical, and powerful. Linear algebra is, quite simply, the language that computers use to perform complex operations on massive amounts of data all at once. Trying to do modern machine learning (like AI, deep learning, or recommender systems) without linear algebra would be like trying to build a skyscraper with a handheld screwdriver. It's just not the right tool.

The Paradigm Shift: From Spreadsheets to Matrices

The first and most important leap of intuition is to stop seeing your data as a spreadsheet (a collection of rows and columns) and start seeing it as one single object: a matrix.

Let's call our main dataset (all our customers and their attributes) a matrix, X.

In this matrix X, every row is a vector that represents one observation (e.g., one user).

In this matrix X, every column is a vector that represents one feature (e.g., "Age").

A vector is just a list of numbers, but more importantly, it's a point in a high-dimensional space. A user vector might look like [Age: 34, Income: 85000, Hours_on_Site: 4.5]. This "user" exists as a single point in a 3-dimensional "feature space."

Why is this useful? Because now we can use math to find distance. A user who is similar to this user will have a vector that is very close to theirs in this space (e.g., [Age: 35, Income: 88000, Hours_on_Site: 4.7]). A totally different user (e.g., [Age: 19, Income: 20000, Hours_on_Site: 1.2]) will be very far away. This is the mathematical foundation of all "customer segmentation" and "k-nearest-neighbors" algorithms.

How Linear Algebra Powers Modern AI

This "data as-a-matrix" framework is what allows for the stunning speed and power of modern machine learning.

Application 1: Recommendation Systems (like Netflix)

How does Netflix know you'll like Stranger Things? It's all linear algebra.

Imagine a massive matrix. The rows are all Netflix's users (let's say 200 million). The columns are all its movies/shows (let's say 50,000).

Most of this matrix is empty. The cells are blank because you haven't seen 99% of the content. The few cells that are filled have your ratings (1-5 stars).

The entire goal of the recommendation system is to predict what numbers to put in those blank cells.

It does this with a technique called Matrix Factorization. This is a core linear algebra concept. The algorithm "factors" this one giant, sparse U×M matrix into two smaller, "latent" matrices:

A User-Feature matrix (e.g., U×k). This matrix "discovers" the latent tastes of every user. (e.g., User 12 is 80% "Action," 10% "Comedy," 10% "Romance").

A Movie-Feature matrix (e.g., M×k). This matrix "discovers" the latent attributes of every movie. (e.g., Die Hard is 95% "Action," 5% "Comedy," 0% "Romance").

The system discovers these "features" (Action, Comedy, etc.) on its own. It just learns that people who like Die Hard also tend to like Lethal Weapon, and it creates a "feature" to represent that similarity.

To predict your rating for a movie you haven't seen, it just takes your "user vector" and the "movie vector" and multiplies them (using a "dot product"). This gives a single number—your predicted rating.

Application 2 (Case Study): Image Data as Matrices

This is the most tangible example. To a computer, a digital image is a matrix.

A simple 8×8 grayscale image is nothing more than an 8×8 matrix of numbers. Each cell is a value from 0 (pure black) to 255 (pure white).

A color image? It's just three matrices (Red, Green, Blue) stacked on top of each other.

How does an AI model in medical imaging diagnose a tumor from a scan? It's not "looking" at the picture. It's performing matrix operations. The AI (a "Convolutional Neural Network") uses "filters"—which are themselves tiny matrices—and multiplies them across the image matrix, over and over. This process automatically learns to detect edges, then shapes, then textures, and finally, complex objects like a "malignant mass."

This is the required foundation. As a data scientist, you may never need to invert a matrix by hand again in your life. But you must have the intuition. You need to know why your model is slow (maybe you're running a loop instead of a vectorized matrix operation). You need to know why your model is failing (maybe your matrix is "non-invertible"). This mathematical fluency is the non-negotiable prerequisite for creating, debugging, and truly understanding the advanced algorithms that shape our world.

3.1 Python for Data Science: Environment and Fundamentals

Welcome to the starting line. Before you can analyze data, you have to build your workshop. In data science, that workshop is your programming environment, and the primary tool is Python. This module is your complete introduction to setting up a professional-grade workstation and mastering the fundamental grammar of the Python language.

Core Knowledge: The Grammar of Python

Think of Python as the lingua franca of data. It's not just a programming language; it's an ecosystem. Its dominance comes from its simple, readable syntax and the vast collection of specialized libraries built by the community. Before we can use those powerful libraries, however, we must understand the core language itself.

This isn't about becoming a software engineer. It's about becoming a data professional who can script. We will focus on the practical fundamentals:

Variables: The "boxes" where you store information. This could be a number (like age = 30), a piece of text (like customer_name = "Sarah"), or a true/false value (is_churned = True).

Data Structures: These are the "shelves" and "file cabinets" for organizing your variables. We will live and breathe three of them:

Lists: An ordered collection of items, like a shopping list. You can add to it, remove from it, and it stays in order. Example: scores = [88, 92, 75].

Dictionaries: The most important one for data work. This is a collection of key-value pairs, like a real dictionary. Instead of looking up by an index number, you look up by a name (the key). Example: customer = {'id': 101, 'name': 'Sarah', 'age': 30}. This is how most data (like JSON from a web API) will arrive.

Tuples: Similar to lists, but they are immutable (they can't be changed). You'll see them used for data that shouldn't be altered, like coordinates: location = (40.7128, -74.0060).

Loops: The engine of repetition. Loops allow you to perform an action on every single item in a list or dictionary without writing the code thousands of times. The for loop is your workhorse: for score in scores: print(score).

Functions: The secret to reusable, clean code. A function is a block of code you can name and "call" whenever you need it. Instead of writing the same five lines of code to clean a customer's name every time, you write one function called clean_name() and use it.

We also introduce the Jupyter Notebook. This is not just a tool; it's a new way of working. It's an interactive, web-based document that lets you write and run code, write explanatory text, and display visualizations all in one place. It's a "lab notebook" for the 21st century, and it's the standard for exploratory data analysis because it lets you see your code, your output, and your thoughts side-by-side.

Updated Application: A Foundational Data Cleaning Script

Let's make this real. Your first project isn't a "Hello, World!" program. It's a miniature version of a task you will do every day.

We'll start with a messy text file, raw_customer_data.txt. Each line might look like this: 101, sarah. jones , 30, NY 102,mike_smith, 25, ca 103, JENNA-BROWN, , FL

The data is dirty. It has extra spaces, inconsistent capitalization, and missing values (the blank ,,). Your task is to write a single Python script that does the following:

Opens and Reads: Uses a with open() statement to read the raw_customer_data.txt file line by line.

Loops and Manipulates: Uses a for loop to process each line. Inside that loop, you will:

Remove leading/trailing spaces (.strip()).

Split the line into a list of items (.split(',')).

Clean the name: remove extra spaces, and capitalize it properly (e.g., sarah. jones becomes Sarah Jones).

Standardize the state: make "ca" and "NY" into "CA" and "NY" (.upper()).

Handle the missing age: check if the age field is empty and replace it with a placeholder like NULL.

Writes and Exports: Takes this newly cleaned data and writes it to a new file, cleaned_customer_data.csv, a format you can open in any spreadsheet program.

This simple exercise teaches you file I/O, string manipulation, and list processing. You have just performed your first "Extract, Transform, Load" (ETL) task.

🚀 Real-Time Case Study: Setting Up the 2025 Analytics Workstation

The most common point of failure for new analysts is their own computer. A project that works for you might fail for your colleague because you have "different Pythons" or different library versions. This is chaos. The "2025 Analytics Workstation" is built on reproducibility using the Anaconda distribution.

Anaconda is a free, all-in-one package. When you install it, you get Python, the Jupyter Notebook, and all the essential libraries (Pandas, NumPy, etc.) at once.

But its real power is conda, its package manager. This is our focus. We will walk through how to use it to create virtual environments.

A virtual environment is an isolated, self-contained "bubble" for each of your projects.

Best Practice: Project A (Churn Analysis) might need an old version of a library. Project B (New Web Scraper) needs the newest version. Without environments, installing one breaks the other.

The conda Workflow: We'll open the Anaconda Prompt (a terminal) and run these commands, which are now industry-standard practice:

Create an environment: conda create -n churn_project python=3.10 pandas This command creates a new, empty "bubble" named churn_project, installs Python 3.10 and Pandas only inside it, and automatically handles all the dependencies.

Activate the environment: conda activate churn_project Your terminal prompt will change, showing (churn_project). You are now "inside" that bubble. Any libraries you install only go here. Your "base" Python is untouched and safe.

Manage: conda install scikit-learn (Adds a new library to the active environment) conda deactivate (Exits the bubble and returns to base) conda env list (Shows all your environments)

This practice is non-negotiable in a professional setting. It keeps your projects separate, clean, and, most importantly, shareable.

📈 Job Skill Enhancement: Python Programming

This skill is the foundation for everything that follows. An analyst who only knows Excel and SQL hits a ceiling. An analyst who knows Python can automate their work, build predictive models, and access any data source. Python's flexibility is its strength. With it, you can write a script to scrape a website, connect to a database, analyze a 10-gigabyte dataset, and build a machine learning model, all in the same language, all in the same notebook.

3.2 Data Manipulation with Pandas

If Python is the workshop, Pandas is your primary workbench. It's the most crucial, most-used library in the entire data science ecosystem. I can't overstate this: proficiency in Pandas is the single most important technical skill for a data analyst. It's the "Excel on steroids" that can handle millions of rows as easily as Excel handles a thousand.

Core Knowledge: The DataFrame

Pandas gives us two new data structures that will replace Python's lists and dictionaries for 99% of your data work.

Series (1D): Think of this as a single column in a spreadsheet. It's a 1D array with labels (an "index"). For example, a Series could hold the age for all your customers.

DataFrame (2D): This is the main event. A DataFrame is the object you will use every day. It's a 2D table, just like a spreadsheet or a SQL table, with rows and columns. Each column in a DataFrame is a Series.

Our entire module is focused on becoming fluent in manipulating this DataFrame object. We'll learn the essential "verbs" of data manipulation:

Import/Export: Reading data into a DataFrame is a one-line command: pd.read_csv('filename.csv') or pd.read_excel('filename.xlsx'). Saving your work is just as easy: df.to_csv('output.csv').

Indexing and Slicing: This is how you "ask for" data. It's the single biggest hurdle for new users, so we focus on the two modern methods:

.loc[]: Selects data by its label (the row index name and the column name). Example: df.loc[101, 'age'] (gets age for customer 101).

.iloc[]: Selects data by its integer position (the row and column number). Example: df.iloc[0, 2] (gets the data in the 1st row, 3rd column).

Handling Missing Data: Real data is messy. df.dropna() will drop rows with missing values. df.fillna(0) will fill them with a zero.

Combining: You'll get data from multiple sources. pd.merge() and pd.concat() are the tools to "join" or "stack" these datasets into one master DataFrame.

The groupby() Function: This is the most powerful tool in Pandas. It's the engine for aggregation. It allows you to split your data into groups, apply a function to each group, and combine the results.

Updated Application: Wrangling a Multi-File Dataset

This project simulates a common business request. You are given three separate files:

sales_2025.csv (contains order_id, customer_id, date, total_amount)

customers.csv (contains customer_id, customer_name, region)

products.csv (contains order_id, product_sku, quantity)

The data is a mess. The sales_2025 file has a 'total_amount' column, but customers has a 'region' column with different capitalizations ('north', 'North', 'N-west'). Your task is to "wrangle" this data to produce a single, clean summary table.

Load: Read all three CSVs into three different DataFrames: sales_df, customers_df, products_df.

Clean: In customers_df, standardize the 'region' column.

Merge: Use pd.merge() to combine sales_df and customers_df on the customer_id column. This "joins" the two tables, bringing the 'region' information into your main sales table. This creates a new master_df.

Group & Aggregate: Use the powerhouse groupby() method on master_df to answer a business question: "What were the total sales for each region?" regional_sales = master_df.groupby('region')['total_amount'].sum()

Pivot: Finally, you'll use pd.pivot_table() to create a clean, presentation-ready summary that shows sales by region, broken down by month.

This project takes you from three messy, separate files to a single, insightful summary table, all using the core Pandas toolkit.

🚀 Real-Time Case Study: Analyzing Telecom Churn Data

Let's use the famous "Telco Customer Churn Dataset" from Kaggle. This is a classic dataset that contains customer demographics, services they've signed up for, and a final column: Churn ('Yes' or 'No'). As soon as we load this data (df = pd.read_csv('telco_churn.csv')), a manager will walk over and ask questions. We can answer them in seconds.

Q: "What's our overall churn rate?"

Pandas:
print(df['Churn'].value_counts(normalize=True))

Answer: This one line of code calculates the percentage of 'Yes' and 'No' values. We can immediately see a result like No: 73.5%, Yes: 26.5%. We've just established our baseline metric.

Q: "Okay, are our long-term customers loyal? What's the average tenure for churned vs. non-churned customers?"

Pandas: print(df.groupby('Churn')['tenure'].mean())

Answer: This splits the DataFrame into two groups (Yes/No), then grabs the 'tenure' column (months with company) for each, and calculates the average. We'll see something like: Churn No 37.5 months Yes 17.9 months

Insight: We've instantly verified a critical hypothesis: churned customers are, on average, much newer.

Q: "I have a feeling our new fiber-optic internet is the problem. Are people with fiber more likely to churn than those with DSL?"

Pandas:
print(df.groupby('InternetService')['Churn'].value_counts(normalize=True))

Answer: This groups by 'InternetService' (which has values like 'Fiber optic', 'DSL', 'No') and shows the churn breakdown for each. We might see that Fiber optic has a 40% churn rate, while DSL only has 18%.

Insight: We've found a "hotspot." The problem isn't all internet; it's specifically fiber. This is an actionable insight you can take to the product team, and it took you 10 seconds to find.

Job Skill Enhancement: Data Manipulation & Wrangling

This is it. This is the skill. Proficiency in Pandas is non-negotiable for 99% of data jobs in 2025. Before any fancy machine learning or beautiful visualization, the data must be cleaned, shaped, and prepared. This preparation, or "wrangling," is 80% of the job, and Pandas is the tool you will use to do it. When a job description lists "Python," they mean "Pandas."

3.3 Numerical Computing with NumPy

If Pandas is the workbench, NumPy (Numerical Python) is the high-performance engine underneath it. You will rarely use NumPy directly for data analysis—Pandas has made it user-friendly. However, understanding NumPy is what separates a basic analyst from an advanced one. It's the foundation that makes all of scientific Python fast.

Core Knowledge: The ndarray

NumPy's core object is the n-dimensional array, or ndarray. On the surface, it looks like a Python list. The difference is what's under the hood.

A Python list is a collection of pointers to objects. A NumPy array is a single, contiguous block of memory. All items in the array must be the same data type (e.g., all 64-bit integers).

Why does this matter? Speed.

Because the data is in one chunk of memory, NumPy can perform "vectorized" operations. Instead of a Python for loop, which processes one item at a time (slow), NumPy can run a single mathematical operation across the entire array at once, often using pre-compiled C code.

This module covers:

Array Creation: np.array(), np.zeros(), np.ones(), np.arange().

Mathematical Operations: Standard math (+, -, *) works on entire arrays at once.

Indexing and Slicing: Similar to lists, but more powerful, allowing you to slice in multiple dimensions.

Broadcasting: This is the magic. Broadcasting is NumPy's set of rules for performing operations on arrays of different shapes. For example, you can add a single number (a 0D array) to a 1-million-element 1D array, and NumPy will "broadcast" that number, adding it to every single element.

💻 Updated Application: The Power of Vectorization

This application is a direct, stunning demonstration of why NumPy exists.

The Task: We have two arrays, a and b, each containing one million random numbers. We need to calculate a complex formula for every pair of numbers, for example, the "Mean Absolute Error" (MAE).

Method 1: The "Slow" Python Loop We would write a for loop to iterate one million times.

Python

```
total_error = 0
for i in range(1_000_000):
    total_error += abs(a[i] - b[i])  # Python 'abs'
```

```
mae = total_error / 1_000_000
```

On a modern laptop, this will take a noticeable amount of time—perhaps several seconds.

Method 2: The "Fast" Vectorized NumPy Way With NumPy, we don't write a loop. We write one line that operates on the entire one-million-element arrays at once.
Python

```python
import numpy as np
mae = np.mean(np.abs(a - b)) # NumPy 'np.abs'
```

This operation is nearly instantaneous. The a - b part is vectorized, np.abs() is vectorized, and np.mean() is vectorized. This isn't just a 10% speedup; it's often a 100x to 1000x speedup.

This is the power of vectorization. When you call df['age'].mean() in Pandas, what's happening under the hood is that the Pandas Series (which is built on a NumPy array) is calling a highly-optimized NumPy function.

🚀 Real-Time Case Study: Image Processing with NumPy

This case study proves that a NumPy array isn't just for numbers—it's for any data that can be represented numerically. An image is a perfect example.

An image is just a grid of pixels. We can load an image (using a library like matplotlib or Pillow) directly into a NumPy ndarray.

A grayscale image is a 2D array. The shape might be (1080, 1920). Each value in the array is an integer from 0 (black) to 255 (white).

A color (RGB) image is a 3D array. The shape would be (1080, 1920, 3). This is 1080 rows, 1920 columns, and 3 "layers" (one 2D array for Red, one for Green, one for Blue).

Once the image is a NumPy array, we can perform "image processing" using only array operations.

Task 1: Crop the image.

Operation: This is just a 2D array slice. To crop the center of the image, we don't need a "crop tool." We just slice the array.

Code: cropped_img = img_array[200:800, 300:1600]

Task 2: Flip the image horizontally.

Operation: We need to reverse the order of the columns.

Code: flipped_img = img_array[:, ::-1, :] (This slice means: "take all rows, reverse all columns, take all color channels").

Task 3: Change the brightness.

Operation: Brightness is just the value of the pixels. To make the image brighter, we add a constant value to every single pixel in the array. This is a perfect example of broadcasting.

Code: brighter_img = img_array + 50

(NumPy is smart enough to "clip" the values at 255, so they don't "wrap around".)

This case study shows how NumPy's abstract tools (slicing, broadcasting) are the engine for powerful, high-performance applications.

Job Skill Enhancement: Numerical Computing

You will likely never be hired for a job that lists "NumPy" as the primary skill. You will, however, be expected to understand it. Knowing NumPy is the key to performance. When your Pandas operation is too slow, you will use NumPy to "vectorize" it and make it fast. It's the foundation that makes the entire "PyData" (Python Data) stack possible, and all the advanced libraries (Pandas, Scikit-learn, TensorFlow) are built directly on top of it.

3.4 Introduction to Statistical Modeling with Scikit-learn

We have set up our environment (Python/Anaconda), learned to wrangle data (Pandas), and understood the high-performance engine (NumPy). Now, we can finally do the "science" part of data science. Scikit-learn (or sklearn) is the gold standard for "traditional" machine learning in Python. It's the library you use to make predictions.

Core Knowledge: The sklearn API

Scikit-learn's genius is not in its algorithms (though they are robust and efficient). Its genius is its simple, unified API (Application Programming Interface). Once you learn the "pattern" for one model, you know the pattern for all of them. This allows you to "try out" a dozen different models with minimal code changes.

The API boils down to three main "verbs" on a "model" object:

fit(X, y): This is the "train" verb. You pass it your features (the data you want it to learn from, X) and your target (the answer you want it to predict, y). The .fit() method is what does all the complex math, "learning" the patterns that connect X to y.

predict(X_new): This is the "predict" verb. After the model is trained (fit), you give it new, unseen data (X_new), and it returns its best guess for the answers.

transform(X): This is the "preprocess" verb. We often use sklearn to clean our data before modeling. For example, StandardScaler().fit_transform(X) will scale all your features to have a mean of 0 and a standard deviation of 1, a common requirement for many models.

This module also covers the essential process of model validation. You never train and test your model on the same data. We use train_test_split() to divide our data into a training set (for the .fit() method) and a testing set (to evaluate its performance on unseen data). This is the single most important concept in predictive modeling to avoid "overfitting."

Updated Application: Your First Machine Learning Prototype

This project is the capstone that ties all the subtopics together. We will build a complete, end-to-end machine learning prototype. We'll use a simple "Housing Prices" dataset, where we have 10 features (like square_footage, num_bedrooms, age_of_house) and one target: price.

Load & Prepare (Pandas): Load the housing.csv into a Pandas DataFrame.

Define X and y (Pandas/NumPy):

X = df[['square_footage', 'num_bedrooms', 'age_of_house']] (Our features)

y = df['price'] (Our target)

Split the Data (Scikit-learn):

from sklearn.model_selection import train_test_split

X_train, X_test, y_train, y_test = train_test_split(X, y, test_size=0.2)

This holds back 20% of the data in X_test and y_test for a fair evaluation.

Train the Model (Scikit-learn):

from sklearn.linear_model import LinearRegression (This is a "regression" problem because we are predicting a continuous number, price.)

model = LinearRegression() (Create the model object)

model.fit(X_train, y_train) (Train the model on the training data)

Evaluate the Model (Scikit-learn):

from sklearn.metrics import r2_score

predictions = model.predict(X_test) (Make predictions on the unseen test data) score = r2_score(y_test, predictions) (Compare the true prices to our predicted prices)

print(f"Our model's R-squared score is: {score}")

In just 10-15 lines of code, you have built a complete, working machine learning model. You've loaded, prepared, split, trained, and evaluated it.

🚀 Real-Time Case Study: Prototyping a "Churn Predictor"

Let's return to our Telco Churn dataset from Subtopic 3.2. We already did the analysis (Pandas groupby). Now, we want to do prediction. We want to build a model that can look at a new customer and give us a "probability of churning."

This is a classification problem (the answer is a category: 'Yes' or 'No'), so we will use LogisticRegression.

The goal here is not to build the best model. The goal is to build a "baseline model." A baseline is the simplest possible model you can build. It serves as a critical benchmark. If your complex, 10-hour-training "deep learning" model can't beat this simple, 5-second LogisticRegression model, then your complex model is a failure.

Prep (Pandas/sklearn): We load the data. We must convert categorical features like 'InternetService' (Fiber, DSL) into numbers using OneHotEncoder from sklearn. We define X (all features) and y (the 'Churn' column).

Split (sklearn): We use train_test_split.

Build Baseline (sklearn):

Python

```
from sklearn.linear_model import LogisticRegression
from sklearn.metrics import accuracy_score

# Create and train the simple baseline
baseline_model = LogisticRegression(max_iter=1000)
baseline_model.fit(X_train, y_train)

# Evaluate the baseline
baseline_preds = baseline_model.predict(X_test)
baseline_accuracy = accuracy_score(y_test, baseline_preds)
print(f"Baseline Model Accuracy: {baseline_accuracy}")
```

This baseline model gives us a "score to beat." Maybe it's 78% accurate. Now, the real project begins. We can try a more complex model, like a RandomForestClassifier, and see if its accuracy is higher (e.g., 81%). This baseline model provides the context to know if 81% is good or bad, justifying the added complexity.

Job Skill Enhancement: Scikit-learn

Knowing sklearn is what elevates an analyst from a historical reporter (who only describes what happened) to a predictive modeler (who forecasts what will happen). This is the "playground" for machine learning. While there are more complex libraries (like TensorFlow and PyTorch for deep learning), 90% of business problems (like churn prediction, fraud detection, and sales forecasting) can be solved effectively with Scikit-learn. Proficiency with this library is the key that unlocks data scientist roles and the most advanced analyst positions.

PART II: THE CORE ANALYTICS WORKFLOW

Database Mechanics and Advanced SQL for Analysts

4.1: Relational Databases and Data Definition (DDL/DML)

Welcome to the bedrock of data analysis. Before you can analyze data, you have to understand where it lives and what rules govern its existence. For most analysts, that "home" is a relational database.

Think of a relational database not as a single, giant spreadsheet, but as a highly organized digital filing cabinet. This cabinet contains many different folders, and each folder is designed to hold one specific type of information. In database terms, the cabinet is the database schema, and each folder is a table. A table organizes information into columns (the categories of information, like "First Name" or "Email Address") and rows (the specific records, like a single customer).

The "relational" part is the secret sauce. It means the tables are linked to each other. The Customers table doesn't also contain all their order information; that would be messy and repetitive. Instead, it's related to a separate Orders table. This structured approach, known as normalization, is incredibly efficient. It prevents errors, saves space, and makes the whole system fast and reliable.

To manage this structure, we use SQL, which is split into two main "languages."

The Blueprint: Data Definition Language (DDL)

First, you must build the cabinet itself. DDL (Data Definition Language) is the set of commands you use to define, build, and modify the database structure. These are the architectural commands. You don't use them every day, but when you do, it's for a significant structural change.

The main DDL commands are:

CREATE TABLE: This is the command to build a new, empty table. It's here you define every column, what type of data it holds (e.g., text, number, date), and its rules.

ALTER TABLE: This modifies an existing table. Need to add a new "Phone Number" column? Need to rename the "Email Address" column to just "Email"? ALTER TABLE is your tool.

DROP TABLE: This command completely deletes a table and all the data in it. It's powerful and irreversible.

The most important rules you define during a CREATE TABLE statement are the keys.

PRIMARY KEY (PK): This is a column (or set of columns) that provides a 100% unique identifier for every single row in that table. For a Customers table, this is customer_id. It's like a social security number for that row. No two customers can have the same customer_id. The database enforces this rule.

FOREIGN KEY (FK): This is the magic that creates the "relation." A foreign key is a column in one table that points to the primary key in another table. This is how you link tables.

Let's build that e-commerce database. We start with DDL.
SQL

```
/* This is our DDL for defining the 'blueprint' */

-- First, create the 'parent' table
CREATE TABLE Customers (
   customer_id INT PRIMARY KEY,
   first_name VARCHAR(100),
   last_name VARCHAR(100),
   email VARCHAR(255) UNIQUE
   /* UNIQUE is another 'constraint', like PRIMARY KEY */
);

-- Now, create the 'child' table that links to it
CREATE TABLE Orders (
   order_id INT PRIMARY KEY,
   order_date DATE,
   total_amount DECIMAL(10, 2),
   customer_id INT,  /* This column will be our foreign key */

   /* This line is the 'rule' that links the tables */
   FOREIGN KEY (customer_id) REFERENCES
Customers(customer_id)
);
```

What does that FOREIGN KEY line really do? It establishes referential integrity. In simple English, it means the database now guarantees that you cannot create an order with a customer_id that doesn't exist in the Customers table. I have seen production systems, built in a hurry, that omitted this rule. Six months later, they had thousands of "orphan" orders in their database—orders with no associated customer. They couldn't be billed, couldn't be shipped, and the data was a nightmare to clean up. DDL and foreign keys are your data quality insurance policy.

The Action: Data Manipulation Language (DML)

If DDL builds the house, DML (Data Manipulation Language) is how you move furniture in, rearrange it, and take it out. These are the data commands, the ones you (or the application) use every single day.

The main DML commands are:

- INSERT: This adds new rows (data) into a table.
- UPDATE: This modifies data in existing rows.
- DELETE: This removes rows from a table.

Let's use our new tables. A new customer, Jane Doe, signs up. That's an INSERT.

SQL

```
/* This is our DML for 'manipulating' the data */

-- Jane signs up. This is an INSERT into the Customers table.
INSERT INTO Customers (customer_id, first_name,
last_name, email)
VALUES (101, 'Jane', 'Doe', 'jane.doe@example.com');
```

A few moments later, Jane places an order. That's another INSERT, this time into the Orders table.

SQL

```
-- Jane buys something.
INSERT INTO Orders (order_id, order_date, total_amount,
customer_id)
```

```
VALUES (5001, '2025-11-13', 79.99, 101);
```

Because of our FOREIGN KEY rule, the database checks: "Does customer_id = 101 exist in the Customers table?" It does. The INSERT is allowed. If we tried to INSERT an order for customer_id = 999 (who doesn't exist), the database would return an error.

The next day, Jane realizes she mistyped her name. She goes to her profile and changes it. That's an UPDATE.
SQL

```
-- Jane corrects her name.
UPDATE Customers
SET first_name = 'Janette'
WHERE customer_id = 101;
/* The WHERE clause is critical! Without it, you'd update
*every* customer! */
```

Finally, after a few years, Janette decides to close her account and requests her data be erased. That's a DELETE.
SQL

```
-- First, we must delete her orders (the 'child' records)
DELETE FROM Orders
WHERE customer_id = 101;

-- Now we can delete her main record (the 'parent'
record)
DELETE FROM Customers
WHERE customer_id = 101;
```

This DDL/DML distinction is the first and most critical concept. DDL is the schema, DML is the data. As an analyst, you'll rarely use DDL, but understanding it is critical. It helps you understand the source of your data, its rules, and why it's structured the way it is.

4.2: SQL for Data Retrieval: Filtering, Joining, and Aggregating

This is the heart of the analyst's toolkit. While DDL builds the database, and DML fills it, data retrieval is about asking questions. The entire practice of data retrieval is centered on one powerful command: SELECT.

This module is about mastering the SELECT statement and its various clauses, which act like a set of filters and lenses to turn billions of raw rows into a single, actionable insight.

The Core: SELECT, FROM, and WHERE

This is the basic structure of almost every query you'll ever write.

- SELECT: Tells the database which columns you want to see.
- FROM: Tells the database which table to get them from.
- WHERE: Filters the rows based on a condition. This is your primary tool for reducing the data down to a manageable, relevant subset.

Imagine our Orders table has 10 million rows. We don't want all of them. We just want to see the "big ticket" orders.

SQL

```
SELECT order_id, customer_id, total_amount
FROM Orders
WHERE total_amount > 1000;
/* This query skips all 9.9 million other rows */
```

The WHERE clause is the workhorse. It can handle dates (WHERE order_date >= '2025-01-01'), text (WHERE region = 'Northeast'), and complex logic (WHERE (total_amount > 500 AND region = 'West') OR promotion_code = 'HOLIDAY25').

The Real Power: JOINs

Data is almost never in one table. Your job is to combine tables to answer real questions. You can't find your "best customers" by looking only at the Orders table (which has total_amount) or only at the Customers table (which has customer_name). You need both. JOINs are how you weave them together.

The join clause connects tables based on their shared key (the Primary Key/Foreign Key relationship we established).

INNER JOIN: This is the most common. It only returns rows that have a match in both tables. Think of it as the "intersection." If you INNER JOIN Customers and Orders, you will only see customers who have placed an order. Customers who haven't ordered yet will be excluded.

LEFT JOIN: This is arguably the most useful join for analysts. It says, "Get me everything from the 'left' table (the first one you list), and if you find a match in the 'right' table, bring that data along. If not, just fill in the blanks with NULL."

This LEFT JOIN is how you find missed opportunities. The most famous "analyst query" is finding people who haven't done something.
SQL

```
/* Find all customers who have NEVER placed an order */
SELECT
```

```
    c.customer_id,
    c.email
FROM
    Customers c  /* This is our 'left' table */
LEFT JOIN
    Orders o ON c.customer_id = o.customer_id
WHERE
    o.order_id IS NULL; /* 'IS NULL' means no match was
found */
```

This query asks to see all customers, and for any who have no matching order_id, it returns their name. Boom. You've just generated a high-value list for your marketing team to target. A RIGHT JOIN is the same, but it prioritizes the right table. A FULL OUTER JOIN shows everything from both tables, matching or not.

The Insight: GROUP BY and HAVING

So far, we've only been retrieving rows. But analysts don't deliver rows; they deliver summaries. This is where aggregation comes in.

The GROUP BY clause collapses rows into buckets. You use it with aggregate functions like COUNT() (count the rows), SUM() (add up the values), and AVG() (find the average).

Let's say you want to find the total spending per customer. You don't want 10 million order rows. You want one summary row for each customer.
SQL

```
SELECT
    customer_id,
    SUM(total_amount) AS total_spending,
    COUNT(order_id) AS number_of_orders
FROM
```

```
  Orders
GROUP BY
  customer_id;
```

This tells the database: "Create a 'bucket' for each unique customer_id. As you go through the rows, throw the total_amount into that customer's bucket and add it up. Also, count how many orders you put in each bucket." Instead of 10 million rows, you now have a clean summary: one row for each customer with their lifetime value and order count.

This leads to one final, often confusing, clause: HAVING.

It's simple if you remember this rule: WHERE filters raw rows (before GROUP BY), and HAVING filters summary groups (after GROUP BY).

If you want to find the top customers who have spent over $5,000, you can't use WHERE SUM(total_amount) > 5000. Why? Because at the WHERE step, the SUM hasn't been calculated yet! You must first GROUP BY to create the sums, and then filter those sums with HAVING.
SQL

```
/* The complete analyst's query */
SELECT
  c.customer_name,
  c.region,
  SUM(o.total_amount) AS total_spending
FROM
  Customers c
JOIN
  Orders o ON c.customer_id = o.customer_id
WHERE
  c.region = 'Northeast' AND o.order_date >= '2025-10-01'
GROUP BY
```

```
  c.customer_name, c.region
HAVING
  SUM(o.total_amount) > 1000  /* Filter the final groups */
ORDER BY
  total_spending DESC  /* Sort from highest to lowest */
LIMIT 5; /* Get only the top 5 */
```

This single query is a perfect example. It answers: "Find the top 5 customers from the 'Northeast' who placed an order in Q4 and who have spent over $1,000 with us in that period." It uses every clause we've discussed. This is the non-negotiable skill of a data analyst.

4.3: Advanced SQL: Window Functions and CTEs

If GROUP BY is the analyst's workhorse, Window Functions are the magic wand. This is the skill that separates junior and senior analysts.

A GROUP BY clause has a huge limitation: it collapses your data. If you group by customer, you lose the detail of the individual orders. What if you want both? What if you want to see an individual order and, in the next column, that customer's all-time total spending?

A Window Function performs a calculation across a "window" (a set) of rows, but it does not collapse the rows. It returns the result right alongside the original data.

The syntax involves the OVER() clause, which defines the "window."

PARTITION BY: This splits the data into buckets, just like GROUP BY.

ORDER BY: This sorts the data within those buckets.

Ranking and Value Functions

This is the most common use. Let's tackle that case study: "Find the top 3 highest-paid employees within each department."

Without window functions, this query is a complex, slow, multi-step nightmare. With them, it's beautiful.
SQL

```
/* Create a 'ranking' within each department */
SELECT
   name,
   department,
   salary,
   RANK() OVER (PARTITION BY department ORDER BY
salary DESC) as rank_in_dept
FROM
   Employees;
```

This query tells the database: "First, create 'windows' for each department (PARTITION BY). Inside each window, sort the employees by salary from high to low (ORDER BY). Then, assign a RANK() number to each."

The result looks like this:

name	department	salary	rank_in_dept
Alice	Sales	120000	1
Bob	Sales	110000	2
Charlie	Sales	95000	3
David	Sales	90000	4
Eve	Engineering	150000	1
Frank	Engineering	145000	2
Grace	Engineering	145000	2
Heidi	Engineering	130000	4

(Note: RANK() gives "Grace" and "Frank" the same rank 2, and skips rank 3. DENSE_RANK() would put them both at 2, and Heidi at 3. ROW_NUMBER() would just number them 1-4 arbitrarily. Choosing the right one is key!)

Now, to get the final answer, we just wrap this in a subquery (or a CTE!) and filter.
SQL

```
SELECT * FROM (
    SELECT
        name,
        department,
        salary,
        RANK() OVER (PARTITION BY department ORDER BY
salary DESC) as rank_in_dept
    FROM Employees
) AS Ranked_Employees
WHERE rank_in_dept <= 3;
```

Time-Series and Running Totals

Window functions are also a game-changer for time-series analysis. LEAD() and LAG() are "time-travel" functions that let you pull data from the next row or previous row, respectively.

This is how you do "before and after" or "month-over-month" analysis in a single query.

Example: Calculate the month-over-month sales growth.
SQL

```
WITH Monthly_Sales AS (
    /* First, aggregate sales by month */
    SELECT
        DATE_TRUNC('month', order_date) AS sales_month,
```

```
        SUM(total_amount) AS total_sales
    FROM Orders
    GROUP BY 1
)
SELECT
    sales_month,
    total_sales,
    /* Use LAG() to get the *previous* row's 'total_sales' */
    LAG(total_sales, 1) OVER (ORDER BY sales_month) AS
previous_month_sales,

    /* Now we can do the math in the same query */
    (total_sales - LAG(total_sales, 1) OVER (ORDER BY
sales_month))
        / LAG(total_sales, 1) OVER (ORDER BY sales_month) AS
mom_growth
FROM
    Monthly_Sales
ORDER BY
    sales_month;
```

Readability: Common Table Expressions (CTEs)

Did you see that WITH Monthly_Sales AS (...) in the query above? That's a Common Table Expression (CTE).

As your queries get complex, you start "nesting" subqueries inside other subqueries. This becomes an unreadable mess known as a "query from hell." A CTE lets you clean this up by creating a temporary, named result set.

Think of it as writing a story, step-by-step. A query that used to look like this:

```
SELECT * FROM (SELECT * FROM (SELECT ... ) a JOIN (SELECT
... ) b) c
```

...can be rewritten with CTEs to be perfectly readable:
SQL

```
/* Step 1: Define your first sub-query */
WITH
Customers_From_Northeast AS (
  SELECT customer_id, name FROM Customers WHERE
region = 'Northeast'
),

/* Step 2: Define your second sub-query */
Q4_Orders AS (
  SELECT customer_id, order_id, total_amount FROM
Orders WHERE order_date >= '2025-10-01'
)

/* Step 3: Now, just join your named sets! */
SELECT
  c.name,
  COUNT(o.order_id) AS num_orders,
  SUM(o.total_amount) AS total_spent
FROM
  Customers_From_Northeast c
JOIN
  Q4_Orders o ON c.customer_id = o.customer_id
GROUP BY
  c.name;
```

This is not only 100x more readable, but it's also maintainable. A new analyst on your team can read this and understand the logic immediately. CTEs and Window Functions are the hallmarks of a true, senior-level data professional.

4.4: SQL Query Optimization and Performance

A query that works is good. A query that works fast is a career.

This is a hard lesson every analyst learns. The query you wrote on your 10,000-row sample dataset runs in 0.2 seconds. You're a hero. Then, you run it on the 2-billion-row production database. Two hours later, the query is still running, the database server's CPU is at 100%, and the engineers are sending you angry messages.

Query optimization is the skill of writing SQL that is not just correct, but efficient. It's about understanding how the database "thinks" and giving it "shortcuts" to get the answer faster.

The Problem: The Full Table Scan

The database's default behavior for a WHERE clause is often a Full Table Scan (or "Sequential Scan"). This is exactly what it sounds like: the database reads every single row in the table, one by one, to see if it matches your condition.

If I ask you to find the page in a 500-page book that mentions "Data Definition Language," the "full table scan" is you reading Page 1, Page 2, Page 3... until you find it. It's slow and horribly inefficient.

The Solution: Indexes

The faster way is to use the index at the back of the book. It says, "Data Definition Language: p. 145." You can flip directly to that page.

A database index is the exact same concept. It's a special, separate data structure that the database maintains for a specific column. It maps the values in that column to their physical location in the table.

When you CREATE INDEX ON Customers (region), the database builds this "index book." Now, when you run WHERE region = 'Northeast', the database doesn't scan the table. It looks at the tiny, super-fast index, finds the exact addresses for all the 'Northeast' rows, and retrieves only them. This is called an Index Seek, and it's an order of magnitude faster.

Primary keys are indexed automatically. But you should always add indexes to columns that are frequently used in WHERE clauses or JOIN conditions (like foreign keys).

The Diagnostic Tool: EXPLAIN ANALYZE

So how do you know if your query is using an index or doing a full table scan? You ask the database.

The EXPLAIN (or EXPLAIN ANALYZE in PostgreSQL) command is your diagnostic tool. You put it in front of your query, and instead of running the query, the database gives you its execution plan—the step-by-step logic it will use to get the data.

You'll get a report that looks like this (for a slow query):

```
-> Seq Scan on big_sales_table (cost=0.00..584930.12
rows=10500)
    Filter: (sales_date >= '2025-10-01')
```

That Seq Scan is your red flag. The database is reading the whole table. The cost (an abstract unit of work) is huge: 584,930.

Now, you, the smart analyst, run CREATE INDEX ON big_sales_table (sales_date). You run EXPLAIN again on the exact same query. The new plan:

```
-> Index Scan using sales_date_idx on big_sales_table
(cost=0.43..8.45 rows=10500)
   Index Cond: (sales_date >= '2025-10-01')
```

Look at that. The plan changed to an Index Scan, and the cost dropped from 584,930 to 8.45. Your 45-minute query now runs in 50 milliseconds. This is the single most effective optimization technique you can learn.

The Big Gun: Partitioning

What about when a table is so massive (billions of rows) that even indexes aren't enough? This is common for event or sales data. The "Real-Time Case Study" of an e-commerce platform is perfect. 99% of their queries are for this month's reports. But the Sales table has 10 years of data in it. Why should a query for this week have to sift through a billion-row index?

The solution is partitioning. You tell the database to split that one logical table into many smaller physical tables, based on a rule (usually the date).

So, your Sales table is physically stored as Sales_2024_Q1, Sales_2024_Q2, Sales_2024_Q3, Sales_2024_Q4, Sales_2025_Q1, and so on.
You still query it as one table: SELECT * FROM Sales WHERE order_date = '2025-02-15'. But the database's query planner is smart. It knows that date only exists in the Sales_2025_Q1 partition. It completely ignores all the other partitions. This is called partition pruning. Your query now runs against a table with a few million rows instead of a few billion. This is how large-scale systems stay fast.

Data Collection and Sourcing in the Modern Enterprise

📈 Subtopic 5.1: Sourcing Data from Enterprise Systems and Databases

Core Knowledge

For most established enterprises, the vast majority of high-value data isn't "out there" on the web; it's "in here," locked within the company's own digital walls. This is the internal, proprietary data that powers the business, and it lives in a variety of systems.

The most common home for this data is in production databases. These are typically SQL-based (like PostgreSQL, MySQL, or SQL Server) and are known as Online Transaction Processing (OLTP) systems. Their job is to be fast and reliable for transactions. When you buy a product, update your profile, or post a comment, you are interacting with an OLTP database. This data is the lifeblood of the company's daily operations.

As companies grow, they quickly realize that running complex analytical queries (like "What was the total sales revenue by region for the last five years?") against their live production database is a terrible idea. It can slow the entire system to a crawl, impacting the customer experience. To solve this, they create data warehouses. These are systems like Amazon Redshift or Google BigQuery designed for Online Analytical Processing (OLAP). They are built to handle massive, complex queries that look at historical data. Data is periodically copied (in a process called ETL—Extract, Transform, Load) from the production databases into the warehouse.

Finally, we have the third-party operational systems. These are cloud-based tools that manage specific business functions, such as Salesforce for customer relationship management (CRM) or Google Analytics for web traffic.

This brings us to the central, lived-in challenge for every data analyst: the data silo. The data exists, but it is fragmented. Marketing has its data in Salesforce. Sales has its data in a custom-built SQL database. Finance tracks revenue in an Oracle ERP (Enterprise Resource Planning) system. These systems were often purchased at different times, by different departments, and were never designed to speak to each other. This is the "Data Silo Challenge."

Updated Application

The first job of an analyst is often to be a data plumber, connecting these disparate pipes. In this application, a student will write a Python script to bridge two common silos: a production database and a simple Excel file.

The script will use a library like sqlalchemy (a powerful "Object Relomational Mapper" that can speak to many different SQL dialects) or a more direct driver like psycopg2 (specifically for PostgreSQL). The first step is programmatic connection: the script will take credentials (a host, database name, user, and password) and establish an active connection to the enterprise SQL database.

Next, it will execute a query. This isn't just a simple SELECT *. It's a targeted query, such as: SELECT customer_id, purchase_date, total_amount FROM sales_transactions WHERE purchase_date >= '2025-01-01'. The script will then fetch these results, loading them into a Pandas DataFrame—the primary tool for in-memory data analysis in Python.

But this data is incomplete. A separate Excel file, perhaps managed by the marketing team, contains a list of customer_id values and their corresponding 'marketing_campaign_source'. The script will use Pandas' read_excel() function to load this second dataset into another DataFrame.

Finally, the script performs the "magic" of integration: a join. Using the pandas.merge() function, the student will join the database results with the Excel data on the customer_id column. The result is a single, unified DataFrame. For the first time, the analyst can answer a question that neither silo could answer alone: "How much revenue did we generate from the 'Summer25' marketing campaign?"

Real-Time Case Study: "The Data Silo Challenge"

Let's make this real. Imagine an executive meeting at a mid-sized e-commerce company. The Head of Marketing presents a dashboard from Salesforce showing they generated 10,000 "marketing-qualified leads" (MQLs) last quarter. The Head of Sales, looking at a report from their separate SQL database, says their team only logged 8,000 new leads and that only 1,000 of them converted to actual sales. Meanwhile, the Head of Finance, looking at the ERP, reports that the revenue from new customers doesn't match either of those numbers.

This is the data silo challenge in action. It's not a technical problem; it's an organizational disaster. The company has no "single source of truth." Because the systems are disparate, each department has an incomplete, and often conflicting, view of the customer.

This leads to two critical failures. First, inaccurate analytics: the company cannot accurately calculate its customer acquisition cost (CAC) or customer lifetime value (CLV). They are flying blind, unable to know which marketing efforts are actually driving profitable sales. Second, it creates a poor customer experience. A customer who just spoke to a sales rep might get an automated email from the marketing system trying to "introduce" them to the product, making the company look disorganized and unprofessional. This case highlights that the most difficult part of data integration is often organizational alignment, which must happen before any code is written.

Job Skill Enhancement: Data Integration

The practical skill learned here is Data Integration. This is a core competency that separates a junior analyst from a senior one. A junior analyst can make a chart from a clean CSV file. A senior analyst can find, access, and combine data from three different, disconnected sources to create that clean CSV file in the first place. This skill is part detective (finding where the data lives), part diplomat (getting permission and credentials to access it), and part developer (writing the code to pull it all together). Mastering this skill makes you indispensable in any real-world enterprise environment.

📡 Subtopic 5.2: Data Collection via Application Programming Interfaces (APIs)

Core Knowledge

If enterprise databases are the company's internal data nervous system, then Application Programming Interfaces (APIs) are the external nervous system for the entire internet. An API is the standard, modern method for services to share data with each other in a structured, secure, and controlled way.

The simplest analogy is a restaurant. You (the user) don't go into the kitchen (the database) to get your food. You interact with a waiter (the API). You have a menu of specific requests you can make (the "API documentation"), and the waiter handles the communication with the kitchen, returning only the food you asked for.

The most common type of API on the web is a RESTful API. This is an architectural style that uses standard web protocols. When you want to retrieve data, you use a GET request. When you want to send or create data (like posting a tweet or adding a product to a cart), you use a POST request.

The data returned by these APIs is almost universally formatted as JSON (JavaScript Object Notation). JSON has become the lingua franca of the web because it's both lightweight (easy for machines to parse) and human-readable (easy for developers to debug). It uses simple key-value pairs, lists, and nested objects to represent complex data structures.

Updated Application

In this project, students will move from internal data to external, third-party data. They will use the quintessential Python library for this task: Requests. This library makes interacting with web-based APIs beautifully simple.

The project will involve using a public API, such as the GitHub API (to pull repository data) or a service like the OpenWeatherMap API (to get current weather data). The first step is authentication. Most useful APIs are not fully public; they require an API key. This is a unique string that identifies the user, tracks their usage, and grants them permission. Students will learn to pass this key securely, typically in the "headers" of their request (e.t., headers = {'Authorization': 'Bearer YOUR_API_KEY'}).

Next, the student will make a GET request to a specific "endpoint" (the URL for the data they want). For example, https://api.github.com/users/google/repos.

Once the request is sent, the student must learn to be a "defensive coder." They will check the response code. A response.status_code of 200 means "OK," and the data is available. A 404 means "Not Found." A 401 or 403 means "Unauthorized," indicating a problem with their API key. And a 429 means "Too Many Requests," a critical concept called "rate limiting."

If the request is successful, the Requests library makes parsing the data trivial. The student will use response.json() to automatically convert the JSON text into a native Python dictionary. From there, they can navigate the (often nested) structure to extract the exact data they need, loading it into a Pandas DataFrame for analysis.

Real-Time Case Study: "Using the Google Scraping API"

This case study demonstrates a critical shift in the data ecosystem. Let's say a company wants to track its competitors' pricing on Google Shopping. They could try to scrape Google directly (as we'll see in the next module), but this is extremely difficult. Google is a technology fortress, and it excels at detecting and blocking automated scrapers.

This difficulty has created a new, smarter market: scraping-as-a-service, which is itself an API. Services like ScraperAPI or Bright Data offer a "Google Scraping API." Here's how it works:

Your company (the user) doesn't try to scrape Google.

Instead, you make a simple API call to ScraperAPI's endpoint.

In that call, you just send the Google URL you want to scrape.

ScraperAPI then takes on the entire "arms race" on your behalf. It has a pool of millions of proxies, it uses headless browsers, it rotates user agents, and it has sophisticated, AI-powered CAPTCHA-solving technology.

A few seconds later, it returns the clean, structured JSON or raw HTML from the Google page.

This is a profound shift. It abstracts away the difficulty of scraping and turns it into a reliable, billable service. The company's developers can focus on using the data, not on the complex, time-consuming, and brittle process of getting it.

Job Skill Enhancement: API Integration & JSON Manipulation

The job skill here is API Integration and JSON Manipulation. This is a non-negotiable skill for any modern analyst or data scientist. Internal data (from Subtopic 5.1) tells you what you did. External data from APIs tells you what's happening in the world.

By mastering this skill, an analyst can enrich their internal datasets. For example, when a new user signs up in your internal database, a script can automatically hit the

Clearbit API with their email address. The API returns a rich JSON object with their company name, size, industry, and even their job title. This enriched data is then written back into your enterprise data warehouse, giving your sales and marketing teams instant, automated intelligence. This is the power of API integration.

💻 Subtopic 5.3: Web Scraping Principles and Techniques

Core Knowledge

What happens when data is publicly visible on a website, but there is no friendly API to provide it in a clean, structured format? This is where web scraping comes in. Web scraping is the automated process of extracting data from human-readable web pages. It is the "last resort" of data collection, used when a formal API is unavailable or insufficient.

The core of web scraping involves two steps: downloading the page and parsing its content.

Downloading: A website's content is defined by its HTML (HyperText Markup Language). This is the raw code that a server sends to your browser. We use the Python Requests library (the same one from the API module) to send a GET request to a URL and download this raw HTML text.

Parsing: This raw HTML is a messy, complex text file. It's not useful on its own. We need to parse it, which means turning that text into a structured object that we can navigate. The gold standard for this in Python is the BeautifulSoup library. It takes the HTML text and transforms it into a "soup" object, allowing you to navigate the DOM (Document Object Model). The DOM is a tree-like structure of tags, classes, and attributes that define the page's layout.

Using BeautifulSoup, a student learns to "select" the data they want. For example, they can ask it to find all <h2> (heading) tags, or all <a> (link) tags that have a specific class attribute, or the src attribute of an <img> (image) tag.

Updated Application

This is a hands-on project where students build their first scraper from scratch. The target will be a sample e-commerce website with a list of products.

The first step is manual: inspection. The student opens the website in their browser (like Chrome or Firefox) and uses the "Inspect Element" developer tool. They click on a product's name and see that its HTML looks something like: <h2 class="product-title">Super Widget</h2> They inspect the price and find: <div class="price_container"><span class="price-tag">$99.99</span></div>

Now, they have their map. They'll write a Python script that:

Uses Requests to download the page's HTML.

Feeds that HTML into BeautifulSoup to create a soup object.

Uses soup.find_all('h2', class_='product-title') to get a list of all product title elements. They will then loop through this list and extract the .text from each element.

Uses soup.find_all('span', class_='price-tag') to get a list of all price elements and extract their text.

Handles the "messiness" of data. The price might be extracted as "$99.99". The script must clean this data, removing the $ and " and converting the string to a floating-point number.

Finally, the script will loop through multiple product pages and organize all the extracted data into a clean CSV file, ready for analysis.

This project teaches a crucial lesson: scrapers are brittle. If the website's developer decides to change class="product-title" to class="product-name", the scraper breaks.

Real-Time Case Study: "Real Estate Listing Aggregation"

This project, based on a very common real-world use case, is about creating a proprietary dataset. A student wants to analyze the real estate market in Lisbon, Portugal. The main website, CASA SAPO, has thousands of listings, but it has no public API to download them all.

The student builds a scraper. This scraper is more advanced than the e-commerce example.

First, it scrapes the main search results page to get the URLs for all individual listings.

Then, it loops through that list of URLs. For each listing, it visits the page and scrapes specific data points: the price, the location (neighborhood), the number of bedrooms, the square footage, and the property features (e.g., "has elevator," "sea view").

The scraper saves all this information into a structured database or CSV.

The student has created a new data asset. This dataset, which exists nowhere else, can now be used for powerful analysis. The student can calculate the average price per square meter in different neighborhoods, map the most common amenities, and identify market trends long before official government or industry reports are published. This is a classic example of using scraping for competitive intelligence and market research.

Job Skill Enhancement: Web Scraping

The skill learned is Web Scraping, which is highly in-demand for roles in competitive intelligence, market research, and data acquisition for AI training. This skill demonstrates more than just technical ability; it shows resilience and problem-solving. It proves that an analyst can acquire data even when no easy path exists. In a world where data is a competitive advantage, the ability to create a new dataset from scratch by scraping the public web is incredibly valuable.

🤖 Subtopic 5.4: Advanced Web Scraping (2025): AI, Ethics, and Anti-Bot Evasion

Core Knowledge

The previous module taught us that scraping is brittle. This module teaches us that, at scale, scraping is a full-blown "arms race." The simple Requests and BeautifulSoup combination is easy to learn, but it fails against modern, complex websites. This is the 2025-era reality: "scraping is easy, but scaling is still hard."

Modern websites use two main anti-detection strategies:

JavaScript-Rendered Content: Many sites (built with frameworks like React or Vue) load an empty HTML shell.

The data (like product listings) is then fetched and rendered by JavaScript in your browser. A Requests call only gets the empty shell, not the data.

Advanced Anti-Bot Measures: These include CAPTCHAs ("I'm not a robot" checks), IP-based rate limiting and bans, and "browser fingerprinting," which checks for signs that you're an automated browser (like your screen resolution, fonts, and plugins).

To bypass these, "stealth" techniques are required:

Rotating Residential Proxies: If all your requests come from one IP address (like your server), you are easily blocked. A proxy service routes your traffic through a pool of millions of real residential IP addresses (making your scraper look like thousands of different, real users).

Headless Browsers: To handle JavaScript, you must use a tool that is a browser. Playwright and Puppeteer are "headless browsers"—they are real browsers (like Chrome) that you can control with code, without a visual interface. They download the page, render all the JavaScript, and then you can scrape the final HTML.

Human-Like Behavior: Your script must act human. This means adding random delays, moving the mouse, and scrolling the page before clicking a button.

This module also covers the critical legal and ethical "gray zone." Scraping is not inherently illegal, but it can become illegal. The key is a compliance-first strategy. This means checking a site's robots.txt file (a request, not a law, but good to follow) and, most importantly, its Terms of Service, which is a binding legal contract. Scraping personal data can also violate privacy laws like the GDPR and CCPA.

Updated Application

This module introduces the very latest in scraping: AI-powered, agent-based scraping. The fundamental problem with traditional scraping (even with Playwright) is its reliance on fixed patterns. A human developer must find a CSS selector like div.price.

New tools like ScrapegraphAI are "agent-based" and use Large Language Models (LLMs). Instead of giving the tool a CSS selector, you give it a prompt: "Go to this URL and extract the product name, the price, and a list of all customer reviews."

The AI "agent" then:

Downloads the page's HTML.

"Looks" at the HTML structure (or even a screenshot of the page).

Uses its LLM-based understanding of what a "price" or "customer review" contextually is.

Finds the relevant data, even if the HTML and CSS classes are random or change on every load.

This is revolutionary. It makes the scraper resilient to website layout changes. The developer's job shifts from writing brittle selectors to writing effective natural language prompts for their scraping agent.

Real-Time Case Study: "The AI-Powered Scraping Market"

This case study analyzes the scraping market itself, which is projected to grow explosively. Verified market reports (and my own search results) confirm this trend, with some projecting the AI-driven web scraping market alone to grow from $7.48 billion in 2025 to $38.44 billion by 2034. (Note: My search found multiple reports; some value the total market differently, but all agree on the high-double-digit growth, especially in the AI-driven segment).

This explosive growth is driven by a powerful feedback loop:

Massive Demand: Modern AI models (like GPT-4, Claude 3) are insatiably hungry for data. They are "trained on the internet." Industry analysis suggests that 70% or more of the data used to train large AI models is acquired via web scraping. This data is needed to provide models with diverse, real-world knowledge.

Smarter Supply: As we saw in the "Updated Application," AI is now being used to perform the scraping. This makes the data acquisition process more resilient, adaptable, and scalable than ever before.

In short, the demand for AI training data is fueling the growth of the scraping market, and the supply of scraping services is now being super-charged by AI itself.

Job Skill Enhancement: Advanced Data Collection & Ethical Compliance

The job skill here is two-fold. First, it's Advanced Data Collection, which means understanding this modern, AI-driven "arms race." It's knowing when Requests is enough, when to use Playwright, and when to pay for an API-based service.

Second, and more importantly, it's Ethical and Legal Compliance. As an analyst in 2025, you are not just a technician; you are a steward of the company's reputation and legal standing. The "compliance-first" strategy is paramount. Before you ever write a line of scraping code, you must ask and answer these questions:

Am I scraping personally identifiable information (PII)?

Does this violate the website's Terms of Service? (A high-profile case, LinkedIn v. hiQ Labs, explored this, but the legal landscape remains complex and risky).

Am I putting too much load on their server, potentially causing a "denial of service"?

Understanding these risks and knowing how to navigate them before a project begins is the mark of a true professional. It protects you and your employer from significant reputational and financial harm.

Data Preparation and Cleaning: The Prerequisite to Value

6.1 Data Profiling, Validation, and Standardization: The Foundational Diagnosis

In my experience, the most excitement in a data project is generated by machine learning models and splashy dashboards. But not a single one of those end products has any value if the project skips this first, non-negotiable step: understanding the data. Before we change, delete, or impute a single cell, we must act like a detective at a crime scene or a doctor performing a diagnostic exam. We must simply observe and document. This is data profiling, validation, and standardization.

🏛 Core Knowledge: Building the Data's "Medical Chart"

Data Profiling is the systematic process of analyzing source data to build a deep, quantitative understanding of its structure, content, and quality. When a new dataset lands on my desk (or, more realistically, in my S3 bucket), I don't just "load it and go." I run a profile. This isn't just a .head() or .describe() in Pandas. It's a comprehensive report. For every single column, I need to know:

Data Type: Is Price a number (float) or a string (object)? If it's a string, I know I have "dirty" data, like "$10.99" or "Contact Us," that will break any math.

Cardinality: This is the number of unique values. Is Customer_ID 100% unique? If not, we have a duplicate key problem. Is State 50 unique values, or 500? If it's 500, I know I have "NY," "N.Y.," and "New York" to deal with.

Completeness: How many NULL values are in each column? If Email is 80% missing, our marketing campaign is dead on arrival.

Distribution: What do the values look like? For a numeric field like Age, I'll plot a histogram. Do I see a nice bell curve, or is it skewed? Do I see values like 150 or -5? These are the first hints of outliers.

Data Validation comes next. This is where we stop just looking at the data and start checking it against reality—the reality of the business. Profiling is descriptive; validation is prescriptive. We create a set of "business rules" that the data must follow.

A Price must be greater than 0.

An Order_Date cannot be in the future.

A State code must be one of the 50 valid 2-letter codes.

A more complex, cross-column rule: A customer's First_Purchase_Date cannot be before their Account_Signup_Date.

When a record fails validation, it's flagged. It's not (yet) fixed or deleted. It's set aside for investigation.

Data Standardization is the "Tower of Babel" problem. This is where we transform all our data into a single, uniform format. If we're combining data, this is non-negotiable. One system stores weights in pounds (lbs), another in kilograms (kg). One system uses "Male"/"Female," another uses "M"/"F," and a third uses "1"/"0." Standardization creates the common language. We convert all weights to kg. We map all date formats to the universal YYYY-MM-DD

(ISO 8601) standard. We transform all categorical values ("NY," "N.Y.," "New York") into a single, accepted form: NY.

Updated Application: The Data Quality Report Script

In practice, we automate this. We write a Python script using Pandas that ingests any "dirty" dataset and outputs a "data quality report." This report is a simple DataFrame, but its value is immense. Each row in this report represents one column from our dataset. The columns of this report are:

ColumnName: The name of the field.

DataType: The data type as seen by Pandas (e.g., object, int64, float64).

MissingValues: The raw count of NULLs.

MissingPercent: The percentage of NULLs (e.g., 35.2%).

UniqueValues: The count of unique values (cardinality).

SampleUnique: A list or string of the top 5 most frequent unique values.

MinValue (if numeric): The minimum value.

MaxValue (if numeric): The maximum value.

When I run this on a new "dirty" sales file, I instantly see the problems. Price is an object type. MissingPercent for State is 40%. UniqueValues for Country is 10, and the SampleUnique shows "USA," "US," and "United States." MaxValue for Quantity is 50,000, which seems like a typo. This report is our cleaning plan. It's the blueprint for all the work that follows.

🏥 Real-Time Case Study: The Healthcare Interoperability Challenge

This isn't just a theoretical problem; it's a massive, real-world barrier. In healthcare, data incompatibility can have life-or-death consequences. Imagine a patient who visits Hospital A (using an Epic EHR) and then a specialist at Clinic B (using a Cerner EHR).

Hospital A records a diagnosis as "Diabetes Mellitus, Type 2."

Clinic B records it as "T2DM."

A lab (like Quest) sends results, but it doesn't use words; it uses a LOINC (Logical Observation Identifiers Names and Codes) code like "17856-6" (for an A1c blood test).

An analyst trying to build a regional health model can't even answer a simple question: "How many patients have Type 2 Diabetes?" This is a catastrophic failure of standardization. This is why healthcare data standards are a multi-billion dollar field. Standards like SNOMED CT are enforced to create a universal dictionary for diagnoses (so "Diabetes Mellitus, Type 2" and "T2DM" both map to the same concept ID). LOINC is used to standardize all lab results. FHIR (Fast Healthcare Interoperability Resources) is the new standard for how these different systems must package and send the data to each other. In this field, standardization isn't just "cleaning"—it's the core engineering challenge.

🛠️ Job Skill Enhancement: Data Quality Assessment

The skill here isn't just writing the Python script. The real skill is Data Quality Assessment. A junior person delivers the data quality report. A senior person delivers the plan. They can look at that report and say:

"The Price column is an object because of '$' and ',' characters; we'll need to strip those and convert to numeric. The State column is 40% missing, but our validation check shows it's only missing for Order_Source = 'Web'. This isn't a random problem; it's a bug in the web form's data capture. I'll file a ticket with engineering. For the Country field, we will build a mapping dictionary to standardize all values to the two-letter ISO code."

This skill transforms you from a "data janitor" into a "data detective" and a "data strategist." You're not just cleaning messes; you're finding the source of the leak and creating the architectural plan for a robust, trustworthy data pipeline.

6.2 Handling Duplicate Data: Deduplication Techniques

If data profiling is the initial diagnosis, deduplication is the first major surgery. Duplicate records are one of the most insidious and costly problems in data. They are a silent killer of good analysis. They inflate counts, skew averages, destroy marketing budgets, and erode customer trust. A systematic deduplication strategy is not optional; it's a fundamental requirement for any data-driven organization.

🏛 Core Knowledge: From Exact Matches to Fuzzy Logic

A complete deduplication strategy is a multi-stage process, moving from the simple to the complex.

Exact Matches: This is the low-hanging fruit. We identify records that are identical across all key fields. In a users table, we might look for duplicates on email_address. In a transactions table, we might look for a duplicate transaction_id. This is the easy part, often handled with a simple .drop_duplicates() command or a GROUP BY query. The real question is defining the "key." Is email enough? What if someone signs up with a work email and a personal email? This leads us to the harder problem.

Fuzzy Matching: This is where the real-world messiness lives. Humans don't type perfectly. Data entry systems have different formats. Fuzzy matching implements algorithms to find non-exact matches. For example, it identifies these as likely the same person:

"John Smith" vs. "J. Smith"

"123 Main St" vs. "123 Main Street"

"Sample Company Inc." vs. "Sample Co." The most common algorithm here is Levenshtein distance, which simply counts the number of single-character edits (insertions, deletions, or substitutions) needed to change one string into the other. "Smith" and "Smyth" have a Levenshtein distance of 1.

Confidence Scoring and Merging: We can't just automatically delete every fuzzy match. "J. Smith" could be "John Smith" or "Jane Smith." This is where we create a confidence score. We build a rule:

Rule 1: If Levenshtein_distance(LastName) < 2 AND Exact_Match(ZipCode) = High Confidence (95%).

Rule 2: If Fuzzy_Match(AddressLine1) > 90% AND Fuzzy_Match(FullName) > 90% = High Confidence (95%).

Rule 3: If Fuzzy_Match(FullName) > 80% BUT Different(ZipCode) = Low Confidence (40%). We then set a threshold. Anything above 90% confidence, we can auto-merge. Anything between 70-90% gets flagged for manual review by a data steward. Anything below 70% is treated as a distinct record. This human-in-the-loop system is critical for preventing costly mistakes.

Updated Application: Deduplication in Pandas with FuzzyWuzzy

In our Python workflow, this is a two-step process. First, we handle the easy wins. We define our primary key (e.g., email_address) and run df.drop_duplicates(subset=['email_address'], keep='first'). This gets rid of the obvious, identical duplicates.

Second, we tackle the fuzzy matches. We use a library like FuzzyWuzzy (now often implemented as thefuzz). This library handily implements Levenshtein distance. We wouldn't just match "John Smith" to "J. Smith" using a basic ratio. We'd use a more robust method like token_set_ratio. This method tokenizes (splits) the strings, compares the intersections, and is robust to word order. For example, fuzz.token_set_ratio("John Fitzgerald Smith", "Smith, John F.") would return a very high score (likely 100), even though the strings look very different.

We would apply this to name and address fields, create a "confidence score" column, and then flag all records scoring above our threshold (e.g., 85) as a potential duplicate group. The final step isn't just deletion; it's creating a "golden record." We'd take the cluster of duplicates (e.g., three records for "John Smith") and merge them, taking the oldest signup_date, the most recent phone_number, and the sum of all purchase_amounts.

📈 Real-Time Case Study: Marketing ROI and Customer Data

I've seen this exact scenario play out, and the business cost is staggering. A large e-commerce company has two separate databases that aren't properly synced:

Sales Database (Post-Purchase): CustID: 4512, Name: John Smith, Email: john.smith@gmail.com, LifetimeValue: $1,200.

Marketing Database (Pre-Purchase): LeadID: 9872, Name: J. Smith, Email: john.smith@gmail.com, Source: 'Spring Newsletter'.

This leads to two massive, costly problems:

Flawed Analytics: The marketing team runs a report on the "Spring Newsletter" campaign. They see it generated a "new lead" (J. Smith) who never converted to a paying customer. They mark the campaign as a failure. In reality, it did work—it re-engaged an existing high-value customer. The Customer Lifetime Value (CLV) models are also wrong because John's value is siloed. They are making bad decisions based on bad data.

Poor Customer Experience: John Smith, who has spent over $1,000, receives the "Spring Newsletter" with a subject line: "Welcome! Here's 10% off your first order." This is, at best, annoying and, at worst, an insult. It makes the company look incompetent and erodes the trust of a valuable customer.

Deduplication (in this case, by matching on the email field) solves both problems. The two records are merged. The marketing team now correctly attributes the re-engagement to their campaign. The analytics team updates the CLV model. And John Smith gets a relevant email, like "Thanks for being a loyal customer! Here's an early look at our new collection."

🛠️ Job Skill Enhancement: Data Deduplication

This is a core data wrangling skill that has a direct, visible impact on the business bottom line. The technical skill is knowing how to use FuzzyWuzzy. The advanced skill is in the strategy and critical thinking. It's knowing that matching on email is strong, matching on zip code is weak, but matching on fuzzy(name) + fuzzy(street_address) + exact(zip_code) is very strong. It's the ability to have a conversation with business stakeholders and ask, "What is our rule for merging? What's the business cost of a false positive (wrongly merging two people) vs. a false negative (missing a duplicate)?" This skill directly connects a technical data cleaning task to business reliability, customer experience, and financial accuracy.

6.3 Handling Missing Data: Imputation and Deletion

After profiling and deduplication, we confront the next major challenge: the "holes" in our dataset. Missing data, or NULL values, are an inevitable part of any real-world data project. They can be harmless, or they can systematically bias our entire analysis and lead to completely flawed conclusions. How we choose to handle them—whether to delete, fill, or flag—is one of the most critical decisions a data professional makes. There is no single "right" answer; there is only the "most appropriate and justifiable" method for the specific problem.

🏛 Core Knowledge: The Three Strategies for NULLs

First, and most importantly, a NULL value is not zero. Zero is a number. NULL is the absence of information. That absence is, itself, a piece of information we must investigate. Our strategies fall into three main categories:

Deletion (Listwise/Casewise Deletion): This is the simplest, but most dangerous, option. It involves deleting any row (case) that contains a missing value. This is only appropriate in a few specific scenarios:

The missing value is in a critical, non-imputable field (e.g., in a supervised ML model, the target_variable is missing. We can't use this row for training).

The missing data represents a tiny fraction of the dataset (e.g., < 1-2%) and we are confident it's missing completely at random.

An entire column is mostly empty (e.g., FaxNumber is 99% NULL). In this case, we delete the whole column, not the rows. The danger is that if 10 columns each have 5% missing data, you could end up deleting 40% of your dataset, introducing massive bias.

Imputation: This is the process of filling in the missing values with a plausible substitute. The goal is to preserve the statistical properties of the data.

Simple Statistical Imputation: This is the most common first step. For numeric data, we fill with the mean (average) or median (middle value). Pro-tip: Use the median for skewed data like Income or Home_Price, as the mean will be pulled unfairly by a few billionaires. For categorical data (like Favorite_Color), we fill with the mode (the most frequent value, e.g., "Blue").

Advanced/ML-Based Imputation: This is where we predict the missing value based on other columns. This is far more accurate. (More on this in the application section).

Flagging: This is a crucial step that is often forgotten. Before you impute, you should always create a new binary column (e.g., Was_Age_Imputed) with a 1 for rows you filled and a 0 for original rows. Why? Because the fact that the data was missing might be a powerful predictor itself. Perhaps people who don't disclose their income have different spending habits. A machine learning model can learn this pattern if we give it this flag.

Updated Application: Simple (Mean) vs. Advanced (KNNImputer)

Let's walk through a practical scenario. We have a dataset of customer profiles, and the Age column is 20% missing.

Simple Approach: Mean/Median Imputation We calculate the median age of all customers (let's say it's 38). We then fill every NULL value in the Age column with 38. df['Age'].fillna(df['Age'].median(), inplace=True)

Pro: It's fast, simple, and preserves the overall median of the column.

Con: It's crude. A customer who buys video games and a customer who buys retirement plans both get assigned an age of 38. This flattens the variance and breaks the relationships between Age and other features (like Products_Viewed).

Advanced Approach: Scikit-learn's KNNImputer This is a far more intelligent approach. The K-Nearest Neighbors (KNN) Imputer works on a simple, intuitive idea: to fill a missing value for a row, it looks at the 'k' (e.g., 5) most similar rows in the dataset.

It takes a row with a missing Age.

It looks at the other columns for that row, like Avg_Purchase_Value, Years_As_Customer, and Favorite_Category_ID.

It then finds the 5 "nearest neighbors"—the 5 other customers in the dataset who are most similar across those other features.

Finally, it takes the average Age of those 5 neighbors and uses that value to fill the blank. A young gamer's missing Age will be imputed based on other young gamers, and an older retiree's Age will be imputed based on other older retirees. This is computationally more expensive, but it preserves the statistical relationships within the data, which is critical for building accurate machine learning models.

🕵 Real-Time Case Study: Smart Imputation and the missingno Library

A senior data scientist's first step isn't to impute; it's to visualize the pattern of missingness. We use a Python library called missingno for this.

The Matrix Plot (msno.matrix(df)) shows you a visual of the entire dataset, with white lines where data is missing. Is it a random "static" pattern? Or are there huge horizontal bands of white? Those bands tell me that a specific batch import failed, or a specific user group (e.g., "iOS users") had a bug where no data was collected for 3 days.

The Correlation Heatmap (msno.heatmap(df)) is even more powerful. It shows the correlation of missingness. It answers: "If Age is missing, how likely is it that Income is also missing?" This helps us diagnose the type of missingness:

MCAR (Missing Completely At Random): Pure static. Simple imputation is fine.

MAR (Missing At Random): There's a pattern. Age is missing only for customers from the "Web" channel. This is easily fixed! We just impute using the median Age of only the web customers. This is called "grouped imputation."

MNAR (Missing Not At Random): The most complex. Age and Income are missing together. This implies people are actively choosing not to provide this sensitive data. Here, flagging is essential, and advanced imputation (like KNN or a model-based approach) is required. This diagnostic step dictates the entire strategy.

🛠️ Job Skill Enhancement: Data Imputation

Knowing the .fillna() command is a junior skill. The advanced, senior-level skill is justification. It's the critical thinking that leads to the choice. It's the ability to write a paragraph in your final report that defends your method:

"The Income feature was 22% missing. A missingno heatmap revealed this was MAR, with missingness highly correlated with Job_Type = 'Freelance'. Simple mean imputation was rejected, as the Income distribution was heavily right-skewed. Instead, we used a grouped median imputation, filling missing Income with the median Income from that customer's corresponding Job_Type and

Experience_Level bracket. We also added a Was_Income_Imputed binary flag to serve as a feature for the downstream model, capturing any unobserved variance from this user group."

That single paragraph demonstrates a mastery of the subject, builds trust in your analysis, and is the true definition of this job skill.

6.4 Outlier Detection and Data Transformation: Prepping for Modeling

This is the final checkpoint. Our data is profiled, deduplicated, and the missing values are handled. Now, we must address the "extremes" (outliers) and "shapes" (distributions) of our data. Many powerful statistical and machine learning models come with a critical assumption: that the data fed to them is well-behaved, often meaning it's on a similar scale and follows a somewhat normal (bell-curved) distribution. Data transformation is the process of "pre-processing" our features to meet these assumptions, ensuring our models can learn effectively and aren't thrown off by skewed or badly scaled data.

🏛 Core Knowledge: Outliers and Transformations

Outlier Detection An outlier is a data point that is abnormally far from other points. The very first question we must ask is: "Is this outlier an error, or is it a feature?"

An Age of 500 is clearly a data entry error. It's noise. We must treat it (e.g., turn it to NULL, then impute).

A Transaction_Amount of $50,000 when most are $50 is also an outlier. But is it an error? Or is it a valid whale customer, or even worse, a fraudulent transaction? In this case, the outlier isn't noise; it's the signal we're looking for. We detect outliers using two primary methods:

Visualization (Box Plots): This is my favorite first look. A box plot visually shows the middle 50% of the data (the "box"), the median (the line in the box), and the "whiskers." These whiskers typically extend 1.5 times the Interquartile Range (IQR) from the box. Any data point that falls outside these whiskers is statistically flagged as an outlier. It's a robust, non-parametric way to see the extremes.

Statistical Methods (Z-score): For data that is roughly bell-shaped, we can use the Z-score. This measures how many standard deviations a point is from the mean. A common rule of thumb is that any data point with a Z-score greater than 3 or less than -3 is an outlier. This is great for Test_Scores but terrible for Income, which is not normally distributed.

Data Transformation This involves changing the scale or distribution of a feature.

Normalization (Min-Max Scaling): This "squashes" the data into a fixed range, usually 0 to 1. The formula is (value - min) / (max - min). The absolute smallest value in the column becomes 0, and the absolute largest becomes 1. This is essential for algorithms that use distance measurements (like K-Nearest Neighbors) and for neural networks, ensuring one feature (like Income in the millions) doesn't dominate another (like Age from 0-100).

Standardization (Z-score Scaling): This is the most common transformation. It doesn't put the data in a fixed range. Instead, it re-centers the entire distribution to have a mean of 0 and a standard deviation of 1. This is the default requirement for many linear models (like Linear and Logistic Regression) and Support Vector Machines.

Updated Application: Taming Skewed Data with Log Transformation

A very common real-world problem is highly skewed data. Think of Website_Traffic_Per_Day, Income, or File_Size. Most values are small (100-500 views), and a few are massive (one viral article got 5,000,000 views). If you feed this "long-tail" distribution to a linear regression model, the model will be terrible. It will be obsessed with that 5-million-view article, and its predictions for the "normal" articles will be way off.

We need to tame this skew. The most powerful tool in our arsenal is the log transformation. We don't use the raw views value; we use np.log(views). Or even better, np.log1p(views) (which is log(1 + views)) to gracefully handle any articles that had 0 views, since log(0) is undefined.

Let's see the magic:

log1p(100 views) = ~4.6

log1p(500 views) = ~6.2

log1p(5,000,000 views) = ~15.4

Look at that! The scale of the data has been massively compressed. The difference between our normal articles and our viral one is no longer 5 million... it's about 9. If you plot a histogram of the log-transformed data, it will look much more like a bell curve. Now, our linear model can find a stable, meaningful relationship, and its predictive power will skyrocket.

💎 Real-Time Case Study: Financial Fraud Detection

This case study perfectly illustrates the "outlier as signal" concept. In the fintech industry, detecting outliers isn't a cleaning step; it's the entire goal. A fraud detection model for a credit card company isn't just looking at the Transaction_Amount. It's looking at features we engineer from that amount.

A user typically makes purchases with a mean of $50 and a standard deviation of $25.

A new transaction comes in for $8,000.

We don't just "cap" this outlier. We instantly calculate its Z-score: (8000 - 50) / 25 = 318. This is a massive statistical outlier.

The machine learning model ingests this as a feature: Transaction_ZScore = 318. Other features in the model might be:

Is_New_Geographic_Location = 1 (True)

Time_Since_Last_Purchase_Secs = 4.5

Is_Typical_Merchant_Category = 0 (False) The model, trained on millions of past fraudulent transactions, sees the combination of a massive Z-score outlier, a new location, and an unusual merchant and instantly flags the transaction, declining it and sending a text to the cardholder. Here, the "messy" outlier data is the analytical payload.

🛠️ Job Skill Enhancement: Feature Engineering & Data Transformation

This is the skill that bridges the gap between "Data Analyst" and "Data Scientist." Knowing how to import StandardScaler from Scikit-learn is easy. The advanced skill is knowing which transformation to apply, and why. It's the ability to:

Diagnose: "I've plotted this feature and it's heavily right-skewed. A standard Z-score will be meaningless."

Prescribe: "I must apply a log1p transformation first to normalize the distribution."

Apply: "After the log transform, now I will apply StandardScaler to center the data at 0."

Contextualize: "However, for the Decision Tree model I'm also building, I will not apply any scaling, as tree-based models are robust to feature scale and skew."

This contextual, model-aware decision-making is the essence of feature engineering. It is a mandatory, non-negotiable step for virtually all high-performance machine learning, and it's what separates basic analysis from predictive, valuable, and robust AI.

Exploratory Data Analysis (EDA): Uncovering Initial Insights

7.1: The Principles of Exploratory Data Analysis (EDA)

Exploratory Data Analysis, or EDA, is far more than a mere preliminary step in a data project; it is a philosophy. Coined by the brilliant statistician John Tukey, EDA is an approach, a mindset of curiosity and skepticism. At its core, EDA is the process of "getting to know" your data. It's the very first, and perhaps most important, conversation you have with a new dataset. You don't start by making demands or trying to prove a point. You start by listening. You ask open-ended questions: What are you made of? What are your quirks? Where are you broken? What stories are you holding?

The primary goals of this "conversation" are foundational. First, we aim to understand the data's underlying structure. This is the basic inventory. What are the column names (features)? What are their data types (numbers, text, dates)? How many rows (observations) do we have? Is the data "tidy," or is it a complete mess that needs tobe wrangled first?

Second, we want to identify patterns and relationships. This is where the detective work truly begins. Do sales reliably spike every weekend? Do customers who buy Product A also tend to buy Product B? Is there a subtle, slow-drifting increase in error rates over time? These patterns are the first hints of the insights we're hunting for.

Third, EDA is our primary tool to detect anomalies and outliers. Data is rarely perfect. An analyst's job is to find the "weird stuff." Why does one user have an age of 200? Why is there a $10,000,000 transaction in a dataset of small-dollar sales? These anomalies can be simple data entry errors, or they can be the single most important finding in the entire dataset—a critical system bug or a major fraud case. In my own fieldwork with healthcare data, an "anomaly" isn't just a typo. Spotting a sudden, collective drift in lab results from a specific hospital wing might not be a patient issue, but rather the first signal that a critical diagnostic machine is out of calibration.

Finally, we use EDA to test assumptions and formulate new hypotheses. This is perhaps the most critical function. The business leadership thinks they know their customers. They might say, "Our most valuable customers are high-income urbanites." Our job in EDA is to make the first check. We create a simple plot of "Customer Value" vs. "Income" and see if that assumption holds. Often, it doesn't. The data might show that a quieter, suburban demographic is far more profitable.

This last point highlights the fundamental difference between EDA and its counterpart, Confirmatory Data Analysis (CDA). EDA is exploratory. It's what you do when you don't know the answer. It's like exploring a new forest, map in hand, just trying to see what's there. CDA is what you do after EDA. Based on your exploration, you form a hypothesis ("I believe a river runs north-south through this forest"). CDA is the process of formally testing that specific hypothesis (e.g., setting up a rigorous A/B test).

In the 2025-era, this process has been supercharged. We no longer have to manually check all 100 columns for missing values. Tools like the Python pandas-profiling library can, with a single line of code, generate a multi-page interactive HTML report. This report is a massive accelerator. It automatically provides distributions, correlations, missing value maps, and duplicate row detection. But this automation is a double-edged sword. It can make an analyst lazy. The tool flags 50 "high-correlation" pairs. The skill—the true job enhancement—is not in running the report, but in interpreting it. It's about having the critical thinking to see that the high correlation between "user's shoe size" and "vocabulary level" isn't a meaningful insight, but is caused by a confounding variable (age). The automation handles the drudgery, freeing the human analyst to focus on the creativity and investigation.

7.2: Univariate and Bivariate Analysis Techniques

Once we embrace the EDA mindset, we need a practical toolkit. This is where we get our hands dirty with code and visualizations, breaking down the analysis into its fundamental building blocks. In my experience, analysts who skip this "boring" part and jump straight to complex models almost always fail. You must understand the individual parts before you can understand how they work together.

The first building block is Univariate Analysis, which simply means analyzing one variable at a time.

For categorical variables (like "Region," "Product Category," or "Customer Type"), our main tools are frequency tables and bar charts. We're not asking deep questions yet. We're asking: How many categories are there? How are the observations distributed among them? A bar chart of a "Country" column might immediately show that 90% of our data is from the "United States," with the remaining 10% spread thinly across 50 other countries. This is a critical insight! It tells us we should probably group those 50 countries into an "Other" category to make our analysis cleaner.

For continuous variables (like "Age," "Income," or "Purchase Value"), we need to understand the shape of the data. Our main tools here are histograms, density plots, and box plots. A histogram is the "story" of the variable. Is it a nice, clean bell curve (a "normal" distribution)? Or is it skewed? For example, a histogram of "Income" will almost always be right-skewed; most people are clustered at the low-to-mid end, with a long "tail" of a few very high earners. A box plot is the best tool for statistically identifying the spread (the interquartile range) and, most importantly, spotting outliers.

After we understand each variable in isolation, we move to Bivariate Analysis: analyzing the relationship between two variables. This is where the first real insights emerge.

Continuous vs. Continuous: The classic tool here is the scatter plot. We plot "Age" (X-axis) against "Income" (Y-axis) and look for patterns. Is the relationship positive (as one goes up, the other goes up)? Is it negative? Is it linear (a straight line) or curved? Or is it just a random cloud of dots, suggesting no relationship at all?

Categorical vs. Continuous: This is one of the most common and useful analyses. We want to compare a number across different groups. For example, "Region" (Categorical) vs. "Average Sales" (Continuous). While a bar chart can show the average, I find grouped box plots to be far more powerful. A bar chart might show that "Region A" and "Region B" have the same average sale. But a box plot might show that Region A's "box" is very tight and small (predictable, low-variance sales) while Region B's "box" is huge (volatile sales with huge upside and downside). That is a much richer, more actionable insight.

Categorical vs. Categorical: We often analyze this with a contingency table (also called a cross-tabulation) or a stacked bar chart. We want to see how the groups interact. For instance, "Product Category" vs. "Region." Are "Electronics" more popular in the "East" region than in the "West"?

To accelerate this, modern analysts use the Python libraries Matplotlib and, more commonly, Seaborn. The seaborn.pairplot command is a true workhorse. With one line of code, it generates a grid showing every bivariate scatter plot for all continuous variables and every univariate histogram, all in one visualization.

In our e-commerce case study, this practical application comes to life.

Univariate: We plot a histogram of "purchase value." We immediately see it's heavily right-skewed. This tells us we have two different customer personas: the vast majority of "casual shoppers" making small purchases and a vital few "whales" making huge ones. We cannot treat them with the same marketing strategy.

Bivariate: We create a scatter plot of "items in cart" vs. "total purchase value." We expect a strong, positive line. But what if we then color that plot by "customer type"? We might see that for "New Customers," the line is steep, but for "Returning Customers," it's flat. Insight: Our returning customers aren't adding more items; they're just buying the same things. Hypothesis: We need a "you might also like" recommendation engine specifically for returning users.

This is the practical skill of data visualization and statistical analysis: turning code into plots, and plots into actionable business insights.

7.3: Multivariate Analysis: Dimensionality and Projection

We've explored variables one at a time and two at a time. But modern datasets are rarely that simple. We often face datasets with 50, 100, or even thousands of variables (also called "features" or "dimensions"). This is the challenge of high-dimensionality.

When you have 100 features, you can't make a scatter plot. A pairplot would be a 100x100 grid, completely unreadable. A correlation matrix would be a noisy, overwhelming mess. Our human intuition, which is excellent at understanding 2D and 3D space, completely breaks down. This is what's known as the "curse of dimensionality."

To combat this, we move into the realm of Exploratory Multivariate Data Analysis (EMDA). The goal is to reduce the "variable space" to a lower dimension so we can use our powerful graphical interpretation skills. We need to "compress" the data while losing as little information as possible.

The primary technique we use for this is Principal Component Analysis (PCA). PCA is an advanced projection method, but the concept is beautifully intuitive. Imagine you have a 3D cloud of data points, but it's shaped like a flat pancake. If you look at it from the side (a 2D projection), it will just look like a thin line; you've lost all the information about the pancake's shape. But if you look at it from the top-down (a different 2D projection), you see the full shape. PCA is a mathematical algorithm that finds that perfect "top-down" view.

It does this by creating new, synthetic variables called Principal Components.

Principal Component 1 (PC1) is a new, combined variable that captures the single largest direction of variance (the "length" of the pancake).

Principal Component 2 (PC2) is the next largest direction of variance, but it must be uncorrelated (orthogonal, or 90 degrees) to PC1 (the "width" of the pancake).

In a real-world application, a student might have a customer survey with 20 questions. These 20 features are too many to plot. But all 20 questions are probably just measuring two or three underlying (or "latent") concepts, like "Product Quality" and "Customer Service Experience." When we perform PCA, we might find that PC1 (a weighted combination of 10 of the questions) explains 50% of the data's variance, and PC2 (a combination of the other 10) explains 30%.

This is a massive win! We can now create a single 2D scatter plot of PC1 vs. PC2. These two new variables have "compressed" 80% of the information from the original 20 variables. When we make this plot, we can see patterns that were invisible before. We might see three distinct "blobs" or clusters of customers. We haven't even run a formal clustering algorithm yet, but our exploratory EMDA has already revealed the natural customer segments. We can then investigate: who is the top-left blob? Ah, they are the ones who scored high on "Product Quality" (PC1) but low on "Customer Service" (PC2).

The case study from analytical chemistry is a perfect, extreme example. A spectrograph can give a lab thousands of wavelength readings for a single food sample. It is literally impossible to interpret this with bivariate plots. In this field, EMDA is mandatory. By running PCA, an analyst can reduce those 5,000+ variables down to 2 or 3 principal components that might perfectly separate "Grape Type A" from "Grape Type B." This skill, Dimensionality Reduction, is the essential bridge between foundational EDA and advanced, unsupervised machine learning.

7.4: Communicating EDA Findings and Formulating Hypotheses

This final subtopic is, in my professional experience, the most critical and most frequently failed step of the entire analytical process. A brilliant analysis that is poorly communicated is useless. The most sophisticated seaborn plot or PCA projection has zero business value if the stakeholder doesn't understand what it means and what to do about it.

The most important "core knowledge" here is understanding what the output of EDA truly is. The output is not a final answer. It is not a deployed machine learning model. The output of a successful EDA phase is a set of concise insights, a list of documented anomalies, and, most importantly, a handful of well-formed, testable hypotheses.

This is the "critical thinking" job skill. I often frame this to my teams as the "So What?" Test.

Finding (The "What"): "I made a bar chart, and sales from Brazil are the highest."

Insight (The "So What?"): "...but when I plotted Average Order Value (AOV) by country, Brazil's AOV is actually below average. Our revenue is driven by a high volume of low-value sales."

Hypothesis (The "Now What?"): "I hypothesize that our marketing in Brazil is attracting discount-seekers, while our marketing in other regions (where AOV is high) is attracting premium buyers."

Next Step (The Action): "My recommendation is to launch an A/B test in Brazil, testing a new ad campaign focused on 'quality' against the current 'discount' campaign, to see if we can increase AOV."

See the progression? The analysis moves from a simple observation to a complex, actionable business strategy. This is the real job.

The "Updated Application" for this is the Jupyter Notebook (or similar tools like Google Colab). A Jupyter Notebook is the perfect medium for this kindof reproducible analysis and storytelling. It allows the analyst to create a single document that combines:

The Code: The executable Python code that shows how the analysis was done (providing transparency and reproducibility).

The Visualizations: The Matplotlib/Seaborn plots that show the results.

The Narrative: The analyst's written interpretation (using Markdown) that explains what the plots mean and delivers the "So What?" and "Now What?".

When I hire analysts, I don't ask for a PowerPoint. I ask for their best-annotated Jupyter Notebook. It shows me their technical skill, their visualization skill, and, most importantly, their communication and critical thinking skills.

The Kaggle E-Commerce case study perfectly illustrates this thought process. The analyst doesn't just present a folder of 50 charts. They present a narrative: "I began by cleaning the raw data, where I found and removed 5% of duplicate rows. I then explored the customer distributions and found, unsurprisingly, that most customers are from the São Paulo state. However, the more interesting finding came when I cross-referenced this with purchase value. I formulated a new hypothesis: 'While São Paulo drives volume, I believe customers from a smaller state (like Santa Catarina) are actually our most valuable, with a higher average purchase value.' I then ran the analysis to test this."

This demonstrates exactly what EDA is for. It is the creative, investigative, hypothesis-generating process. It's the ability to look at a chart, translate that visual pattern into a business-relevant narrative, and formulate the intelligent "next questions" that will drive the company forward. This "soft skill" is, without question, the most valuable and most sought-after skill in the entire data ecosystem.

PART III: VISUALIZATION, COMMUNICATION, AND GOVERNANCE

Principles of Data Visualization and Storytelling

Subtopic 8.1: Principles of Effective Data Visualization

The human brain is a marvel of pattern recognition, but it was not designed to read spreadsheets. We are visual creatures, evolved over millennia to spot the tiger in the grass, not to mentally aggregate the third column of a CSV file. This is the entire foundation of data visualization. It's not about making data "pretty"; it's a discipline of translation. Effective data visualization is the act of translating raw, abstract numbers into a visual language that our brains can process almost instantly. It's about clarity, not decoration.

When you fail at this translation, the consequences are immediate. You create confusion, you obscure the truth, and you waste everyone's time. The core skill is knowing which "language" or chart type to use for the question you are trying to answer.

Core Knowledge: Choosing the Right Tool

The principles of visualization are a toolkit for answering questions. Never start by thinking, "I want to make a pie chart." Always start by asking, "What do I need my audience to know?" The answer to that question will lead you to the correct chart.

Bar Charts: These are the workhorses of data visualization. They answer the question, "How much?" or "Which one has more?" They are perfect for comparing distinct categories. For example, you wouldn't use a line graph to compare the sales figures of three different products (e.g., Product A, Product B, Product C). You would use a bar chart. It gives an immediate, clear visual answer: "Product A is the winner."

Line Graphs: These charts are masters of one thing: showing change over time. They answer the question, "How has this evolved?" By connecting distinct data points, they reveal trends, seasonality, and volatility. A classic example is tracking website traffic every day for a month. The line's upward or downward slope is the story.

Scatter Plots: This is your primary tool for investigating relationships. They answer the question, "Is there a connection between these two things?" Each point on the graph represents two numerical values. For instance, you could plot every store's advertising budget (X-axis) against its quarterly sales (Y-axis). If the points form a rough line going up and to the right, you've just visualized a positive correlation.

Maps: The question here is obvious: "Where is this happening?" Maps are essential for any data that has a geographic component. They are unparalleled for showing spatial patterns, like "Which states have the highest concentration of customers?" or "Where are our delivery routes least efficient?"

Bullet Charts: This is a more modern, superior replacement for the gauges and speedometers you see in older dashboards. A gauge wastes an enormous amount of space to show just one or two numbers. A bullet chart, by contrast, is dense and clear. It answers the question, "Are we on track?" It typically shows a single bar representing the current value (e.g., "$75,000 in sales"), a target line (e.g., "$100,000 quota"), and shaded regions for performance (e.g., "poor," "satisfactory," "good").

Beyond chart choice, the design principles are what separate a professional from an amateur. The most important concept, coined by the pioneer Edward Tufte, is the "data-ink ratio." This is the ratio of "ink" used to display data versus the total "ink" in the graphic. Your goal is to maximize this.

This leads directly to the avoidance of "chart junk." Chart junk is any visual element that does not convey data and serves only to distract. This includes:

3D effects: A 3D pie chart is a data visualization crime. The 3D perspective distorts the size of the slices, making those in the "front" appear larger than those in the "back," which is a form of lying with data.

Unnecessary textures and gradients: A bar chart with a wood-grain texture or a shiny, reflective surface adds no information. It is chart junk.

Shadows and outlines: These elements add visual clutter without adding clarity.

Finally, color must be used purposefully. Color is a powerful tool, not a paint bucket. Use it to encode a variable (e.g., in a map, "blue" means low values, "red" means high values) or to draw immediate emphasis (e.g., in a line chart of ten competitors, our company is a bold blue while all others are a muted gray).

Updated Application: The Dashboard Redesign

I've seen this scenario play out dozens of times in my career. A manager presents a "bad" dashboard, and it's a sensory assault. It's cluttered, with five different color palettes, gauges that look like they belong in a 1990s video game, and a massive 3D pie chart dominating the center. The user's eye doesn't know where to look. It's a dashboard that reports numbers but answers no questions.

The redesign exercise is a lesson in applied empathy. We start by critiquing it against best practices:

Is it answering a key business question? (Usually, no. It's just a collection of metrics.)

Is the most important information in the top-left? (Users read dashboards like they read text.)

Are the chart choices correct? (The 3D pie chart is used for 12 categories, which is unreadable. A simple bar chart would be better.)

Is the color use disciplined? (It's a "rainbow" dashboard, which is distracting and looks unprofessional.)

Is it cluttered? (It's full of chart junk, borders, and logos.)

The redesign process is an act of "subtractive sculpting." You remove everything that isn't data. You replace the gauges with slim, effective bullet charts. You swap the 3D pie chart for a clean, sorted horizontal bar chart. You enforce a strict, limited color palette. You align everything on a grid. The final result is often described as "calm," "clean," or "intuitive." The real victory is that a user can now look at it and, within five seconds, understand the state of the business.

Real-Time Case Study: Tableau's Visualization Engine

Tableau's dominance in the market isn't just about marketing; it's about their core technology. Their "visualization engine," often discussed as part of their VizQL technology, is fundamentally different. Most tools make you build a chart. Tableau lets you ask a question.

When you drag a data field (like "Sales") to the "Rows" shelf and another (like "Region") to the "Columns" shelf, Tableau's engine doesn't just run a query. It interprets your intent. It sees a measure ("Sales") and a dimension ("Region") and instantly decides the best visual encoding is a bar chart. If you then drag "Order Date" to the "Columns" shelf, it re-evaluates and changes the visualization to a line graph, because it understands that "Date" implies a time series.

This creates a state of "visual flow" for the analyst. You are not stuck in configuration menus. You are in a real-time dialogue with your data. This engine is also what allows for the high-level customization and interactivity. An analyst can create a dashboard that links multiple charts. Clicking on the "East" region in a map instantly filters the bar chart, line graph, and scatter plot on the same dashboard to show only data for the East. This ability to slice, filter, and drill down interactively, all powered by this sophisticated engine, is what allows analysts to move beyond static reports and build compelling, accessible data tools.

Job Skill Enhancement: Data Visualization

In today's job market, "Data Visualization" is a non-negotiable, fundamental skill, just like "Excel" was 20 years ago. It is listed as a requirement in virtually every data analyst, business analyst, and data scientist job posting.

Here's the lived experience: your analysis, your predictive model, or your deep insight is worthless if you cannot communicate it to a decision-maker. That decision-maker does not have the time or technical background to read your code or your statistical tables. The visualization is the "last mile" of your analytic journey. It is the bridge between your complex finding and their business-changing action.

Being skilled at visualization means you are clear, you are persuasive, and you are valuable. You are the one who can take a complex, messy spreadsheet and, in a single chart, make the entire executive team go, "Ah, I see it now." That ability is a career accelerator.

Subtopic 8.2: Data Storytelling: Crafting Compelling Narratives

If data visualization is the language, data storytelling is the narrative. This is a critical distinction that many aspiring analysts miss. A dashboard full of clear, effective charts is good. It's a good report. But it's not a story. A report informs; a story persuades. Data storytelling is the art and science of weaving data into a compelling narrative that connects with an audience on an emotional level and, most importantly, drives a specific action.

This skill is what separates a junior analyst from a senior strategist. The junior analyst presents a chart and says, "Here are the numbers." The storyteller presents the same chart and says, "Let me tell you why this number matters more than any other on this page."

Core Knowledge: The Structure of a Data Story

At its heart, this is a communication skill, not a technical one. It involves three key phases.

Finding the Story (The "So What?"): This is the exploration phase. It's often messy. You might create 50 charts, run 20 queries, and build 10 tables. Most of them will be dead ends. You are looking for the anomaly, the surprise, the tension. You are looking for the insight. The story isn't "We looked at the data." The story is "We looked at the data, and we found something we never expected." This is the "so what?"—the central point of your entire narrative.

Narrative Structure: A good data story follows the same structure as any good story told for thousands of years: Setup, Conflict, and Resolution.

Setup: This is the context. It's the "world as it was." For example: "For the last three years, our customer retention rate has been steady at 85%." This grounds the audience in a stable, understood reality.

Conflict: This is the "inciting incident." It's the problem, the tension, the "oh no" moment. For example: "But in the last quarter, it suddenly dropped to 78%. This isn't just a blip; it's a significant break from the trend, and it cost us $1.2 million." Now you have your audience's attention. They are worried.

Resolution: This is the "so what?" and the "now what?" You explain the why and propose the action. "Our analysis revealed the drop is almost entirely from one segment: customers on our old 'Pro' plan. They are leaving for a new competitor. Here is our proposed three-part plan to launch a new retention offer to this specific group."

Audience Connection: This is the most crucial part. You must know your audience. A presentation to the engineering team can be technical. A presentation to the C-suite cannot. You must connect the data to what they care about. They don't care about your SQL query's elegance or the p-value of your regression. They care about risk, cost, and opportunity. You must frame your story in their language.

This is the key difference between exploration and explanation. Your exploration is a tangled mess of code, queries, and dead-end charts. Your explanation—the final story—must be a clean, simple, linear path that hides all that mess and guides your audience directly from the setup to your proposed action.

Updated Application: "Speak Human, Not SQL"

I've coached many analysts on this exact transformation. They come to me with a finding, and they're excited. They say, "Look! After performing a cohort analysis grouped by acquisition channel and segment, I found a statistically significant 12% year-over-year revenue decline in the North region, primarily driven by a 30% drop in sales for Product Z."

My response is, "That's a great finding. It's not a story."

We then work to "speak human." We reframe it for a C-suite executive who has five minutes between meetings.

Dry/Technical Finding: "In Q1, the North region saw a 12% drop in revenue compared to last year, mostly due to a decline in product Z..."

Compelling C-Suite Story: "Good morning. Today I'm going to share the story of how a 12% revenue drop in the North revealed a critical insight about a new competitor we didn't know we had. This problem is costing us money, but it's also given us a clear opportunity to fight back and win."

Notice the difference? The first is a fact. The second is a narrative. It has a protagonist (us), a villain (the competitor), a conflict (the revenue drop), and the promise of a resolution (the opportunity). This is what gets stakeholders to lean in, listen, and, ultimately, trust you.

Real-Time Case Study: Airbnb's Data Storytelling

Airbnb is a masterclass in this. Their business is incredibly complex—a two-sided marketplace of hosts and guests, spread across millions of unique locations with dynamic pricing. Raw data from their platform would be an unreadable tidal wave of numbers.

Airbnb's data science team famously excels at transforming this raw data into intuitive, compelling stories. The prompt's example is perfect: "Where is demand highest and host supply lowest?" This is a multi-million dollar business question.

A "bad" answer: A spreadsheet of 10,000 zip codes and their host/guest ratios.

Airbnb's answer: A dynamic, color-coded map. It visually shows "hot spots" of guest demand in bright red and "cold spots" of host supply in deep blue.

This visual story speaks directly to the business challenge. A strategy team can look at this map and instantly know exactly where to focus their next host-recruitment marketing campaign. They don't need to read a 50-page report. The map is the story and the call to action. They use these visual narratives internally to make some of their most important strategic decisions, moving from complex data to "We need to act here."

Job Skill Enhancement: Data Storytelling & Business Communication

As the research from top universities like MIT and UChicago confirms, this is the single biggest differentiator for top-tier analysts. Technical skills (SQL, Python, Tableau) are the barrier to entry. They get you the job. Data storytelling is what gets you promoted.

This skill transforms you from a service department to a strategic partner.

The Service Department Analyst: Waits for a "ticket." Someone asks, "Can you pull the sales numbers for the North?" The analyst pulls the numbers, emails the report, and closes the ticket.

The Strategic Partner (The Storyteller): Pulls the numbers, sees the 12% drop, investigates the "why" without being asked, uncovers the competitor threat, and proactively schedules a meeting with the head of sales to present the story and a solution.

One is a "data-puller." The other is a leader. This ability to persuade, influence, and connect your data to the bottom line of the business is the most valuable and highest-paid skill in the analytics field.

Subtopic 8.3: Visualization with Python (Matplotlib and Seaborn)

While tools like Tableau are fantastic for interactive exploration, creating visualizations programmatically with code is a fundamental skill for any serious data scientist or analyst. Why use code? The two "must-have" reasons are reproducibility and automation.

If you create a chart by clicking and dragging, it's a one-time craft project. If you create a chart with code, you have a recipe. You can re-run that recipe every day with new data. This is how you automate the "Monday morning report." This is how you integrate a visualization into a larger data science workflow, creating a shareable, verifiable record of your work. In the Python ecosystem, this foundation is built on two key libraries: Matplotlib and Seaborn.

Core Knowledge: The Two Pillars of Python Plotting

Matplotlib: This is the foundational library, the "grandfather" of all Python plotting. It is powerful, robust, and gives you low-level control over every single element of your plot. If you can imagine it, you can probably build it with Matplotlib. This is both its greatest strength and its biggest challenge. It can be verbose. You often have to write several lines of code just to get a simple plot, manually defining the figure, the axes, the labels, the titles, and the ticks. You use Matplotlib when you need absolute, granular control for a very specific, often publication-quality, custom chart.

Seaborn: This is a high-level library built directly on top of Matplotlib. If Matplotlib is the engine and chassis, Seaborn is the beautifully designed car body with a smart navigation system. It is statistically-oriented and aesthetically-driven. It's "opinionated"—it comes with beautiful default styles and color palettes. Where Matplotlib requires five lines of code for a basic bar chart, Seaborn often requires just one. It's designed to work seamlessly with Pandas DataFrames. More importantly, it excels at creating complex statistical graphics with ease, like histograms, box plots (for showing distributions), violin plots, and, critically, heatmaps (perfect for visualizing correlation matrices).

The typical workflow I've seen in the field is to use Seaborn for 90% of your exploratory plotting because it's fast and easy, and then drop down to Matplotlib's functions to "clean up" or "customize" the Seaborn plot, like adjusting axis labels or adding a custom annotation.

Updated Application: The "Dashboard" of Subplots

This is an incredibly practical and common task. You've done a deep analysis of a customer segment, and you need to send a one-page summary to a manager. You don't want to send three separate .png files; you want a single, coherent image. This is where Matplotlib's subplot functionality is king.

You start by creating a "grid" for your plots, say, two rows and two columns: fig, axes = plt.subplots(nrows=2, ncols=2, figsize=(12, 10)). This axes variable is now a 2x2 array. You can "target" each element in the array to place a different chart there:

Top-Left (axes[0, 0]): You'd use seaborn.lineplot and pass it ax=axes[0, 0] to show the customer's sales trend over time.

Top-Right (axes[0, 1]): You'd use seaborn.barplot (again, passing ax=axes[0, 1]) to show their regional sales breakdown.

Bottom-Left (axes[1, 0]): As the prompt suggests, you could use matplotlib.pyplot.pie (passing ax=axes[1, 0]) to show their product category preferences. Though, as a quick professional note, a horizontal bar chart is almost always more readable than a pie chart.

Bottom-Right (axes[1, 1]): You could add a seaborn.histplot to show the distribution of their average order value.

Finally, you run plt.tight_layout() to make it all look clean, and fig.savefig("customer_summary.png"). You now have a single, shareable, and reproducible dashboard image that tells a multi-faceted story.

Real-Time Case Study: Visualizing Missing Data

This is one of my favorite "power user" applications of visualization. It's not for a final presentation; it's a diagnostic tool for the analyst. Every data analyst knows the pain of missing data (NaN values). The first step is usually df.isnull().sum() to see how much data is missing.

But this tells you nothing about the pattern of missingness. This is where the missingno library comes in. It's built on Matplotlib and provides a suite of tools to see your missing data.

The Matrix Plot: This is the most valuable. It visualizes your entire DataFrame as a grid. Each row is a row from your data, and each column is a column. It paints a black bar if the data exists and a white space if the data is missing.

When you look at this, you don't just see a number; you see a structure. The example in the prompt is perfect: you might see that a white-space "gap" in Column A (e.g., sensor_reading_1) is always accompanied by a gap in Column B (e.g., sensor_reading_2). This is a massive insight! It tells you that your missing data isn't random; it's structural. Perhaps those two sensors are on the same power circuit and fail together. This discovery, which is purely visual, completely changes how you would handle (or "impute") that missing data. You've found a "known unknown" that a simple sum() would have hidden.

Job Skill Enhancement: Python Visualization

This skill is about adding three critical arrows to your quiver: automation, reproducibility, and integration.

Reproducibility: Your Jupyter Notebook or Python script is a complete record of your work. Anyone (including your future self) can open it, run it, and get the exact same chart. This is the gold standard for scientific and analytical rigor.

Automation: This is the efficiency-multiplier. That "dashboard" of subplots you built? You can put it in a Python script, set it on a server, and have it automatically run every Monday at 9 AM, grab the latest data from the database, and email the new customer_summary.png to the entire sales team. You've automated a core business report.

Integration: This is the most important for data science. Your visualization is not a separate step; it's part of a workflow. You use Pandas to clean data, Scikit-learn to build a predictive model, and then Matplotlib/Seaborn to plot the model's results (e.g., a "confusion matrix" heatmap or a "feature importance" bar chart). This all happens in one environment, one script. This "full-stack" analytical capability is what separates data analysts from data scientists.

Subtopic 8.4: Interactive Visualization for the Web (Plotly and Bokeh)

We've covered static charts for reports (Matplotlib/Seaborn) and interactive charts for desktop exploration (Tableau). The final frontier is creating interactive, web-based visualizations with code. This is the skill that lets you build modern, user-facing data products and sophisticated internal dashboards.

The key shift here is from presentation to exploration. A static chart is a statement: "Here is what I found." An interactive web-chart is an invitation: "Here is the data; what can you find?" This is a massive leap in value. Instead of giving your user a fish (a single insight), you're giving them a fishing rod (a tool to find their own insights). The two dominant libraries for this in Python are Plotly and Bokeh.

Core Knowledge: The Interactive Powerhouses

Plotly (and Plotly Express): This library has become the de-facto standard for creating a huge range of beautiful, interactive, D3.js-based charts. Its high-level API, plotly.express, is a joy to use. Like Seaborn, it often takes just one line of code to generate a rich, interactive chart from a Pandas DataFrame. Its key features are what users now expect from a modern data viz:

Hover-over tooltips: Mousing over a data point reveals a detailed box of information.

Zooming and Panning: Users can click and drag to "zoom in" on a specific area of interest, and double-click to reset the view.

Clickable Legends: Users can click on items in the legend to toggle data series on or off, simplifying a cluttered chart. Plotly charts are "web-native." They are designed to be exported as a single, self-contained HTML file, which you can easily share or embed in a website.

Bokeh: Bokeh is also an incredibly powerful library for creating interactive plots. Where Plotly is often seen as the go-to for "shiny charts," Bokeh is often favored for building more complex, web-based data applications. Its key strength lies in its ability to connect visualization widgets (like sliders, dropdown menus, and buttons) to Python code running on a server (a "Bokeh Server"). This means you can build a dashboard where a user can move a slider, and it doesn't just filter the data in the browser; it triggers a Python function on the server to re-run a model and push the new results back to the plot. This is how you build true, data-driven applications.

Updated Application: From Static to Interactive

This is a fantastic "level-up" exercise. A student first builds a line chart of monthly sales using Matplotlib (from Subtopic 8.3). It's a fine chart. It shows the trend. But if a manager sees a huge spike in March, they have a question: "What was the exact number on that day, and what about the day before?" With the static Matplotlib chart, they have to email the analyst and ask them to look it up.

Now, the student takes the exact same DataFrame and gives it to Plotly: fig = plotly.express.line(df, x='date', y='sales'). The student then saves this as fig.write_html("sales_chart.html").

The result is a total transformation. When the manager opens this HTML file, they can now move their mouse directly over that spike in March. A tooltip instantly appears: "date: 2024-03-15, sales: $125,430". They have answered their own question, with no friction. They can also zoom in on just March to see the day-by-day volatility. The analyst hasn't just provided a chart; they've provided an answer-finding tool. This small enhancement in user experience is a massive leap in perceived value.

Real-Time Case Study: Building Interactive Financial Dashboards

This is the quintessential example of where static charts fail. A financial analyst or trader needs to look at a stock chart. A static .png of a stock's price over the last year is almost worthless. The entire point of financial analysis is to zoom in on different time scales and see granular details.

Using Plotly, an analyst can build a professional-grade financial dashboard.

The Chart: They would create an OHLC (Open, High, Low, Close) chart or a "candlestick" chart, which is a standard in finance.

The Interactivity: This is where it becomes a real tool. The user needs to be able to:

Zoom: Instantly look at the 1-day, 5-day, 1-month, 6-month, and 5-year view.

Pan: Scroll back and forth in time.

Hover: Mouse over any day's candlestick to see the exact Open, High, Low, and Close prices for that specific day.

Range Sliders: Many Plotly charts have a "range slider" at the bottom, allowing the user to visually select a time window to focus on.

This is a scenario where interactivity is not a "nice-to-have"; it is the core requirement. A static chart simply cannot do the job. Plotly (and Bokeh) are built to handle exactly this kind of dense, high-resolution time-series data and make it effortlessly explorable for a demanding user.

Job Skill Enhancement: Interactive Visualization

This skill set is what moves you from being a "back-office" analyst to a "front-end" builder of data products. The demand for this skill is exploding. Every modern company, from tech startups to legacy corporations, is trying to build a "data culture." What does that mean in practice? It means building internal BI dashboards and external data products that allow non-technical users to "self-serve" insights.

When you can build these tools, you are no longer just analyzing the business; you are building the tools that the entire business uses to make decisions. This role is often a hybrid between a data analyst, a data engineer, and a software developer. It's a high-demand, high-impact position. Being the person who can "build that interactive dashboard everyone loves" makes you one of the most visible and valuable data professionals in any organization.

Business Intelligence Tools and Enterprise Reporting

9.1 Enterprise Business Intelligence with Microsoft Power BI

When we talk about enterprise-level business intelligence, it's almost impossible to have that conversation without immediately mentioning Microsoft Power BI. For many organizations, especially those already running on a Microsoft-based infrastructure, Power BI has become the de facto language of data. It's not just a single tool; it's a complete ecosystem designed to handle the entire BI workflow, from raw data connection to executive-level collaboration.

This ecosystem is built on three core components:

Power BI Desktop: This is the command center, the authoring tool where the heavy lifting happens. It's a free application for Windows where analysts and developers connect to an incredibly wide array of data sources. You can pull in a simple Excel file, connect to an on-premise SQL Server database, or link directly to cloud services like Azure Synapse Analytics or Salesforce. This is where you clean and transform that data using the Power Query engine, build a relational data model (which is the "brain" behind the report), and create your visualizations.

Power BI Service: Once your report is built in Desktop, you publish it to the Power BI Service. This is the cloud-based (SaaS - Software as a Service) hub for sharing and collaboration. This is where reports become live dashboards. You can set up automatic data refreshes, share reports with colleagues inside and outside your organization, and organize content into "workspaces" for different teams (e.g., Sales, Finance, Operations).

Power BI Mobile: This component does exactly what it sounds like—it makes your reports and dashboards accessible on iOS and Android devices. This is crucial for operational leaders and field-based teams who need to make decisions on the go, not just when they're at their desks.

The "Updated Application" for this module perfectly illustrates this workflow. An analyst is tasked with building a complete sales dashboard. They open Power BI Desktop and connect to two different sources: a local Excel file containing sales targets and a live Azure SQL database holding real-time transaction data. They use the modeling view to create a relationship between these tables (e.g., linking them on a 'Date' or 'Employee ID' key). They then build several report pages with interactive charts, maps, and tables. Crucially, they add slicers (dynamic filters), so a manager can click a button to see performance for just "North America" or "Q4." Finally, they hit "Publish," and that report is now live in the Power BI Service, accessible via a web browser or mobile app for the entire management team.

Real-Time Case Study: The Power BI 2025-2026 Advantage

This brings us to the "why." Why would a large enterprise, faced with many options, standardize on Power BI? The 2025-2026 case study highlights three massive advantages.

First is cost-effectiveness. This is, without a doubt, Power BI's single biggest competitive weapon. For organizations already paying for a Microsoft 365 E5 license, Power BI Pro is often included. Even for other license tiers, the per-user cost is dramatically lower than its main competitors. This isn't just a small discount; it's a fundamental difference in pricing philosophy that makes it feasible to roll out BI to everyone in the company, not just a select team of analysts.

Second is the seamless integration with the Microsoft stack. This is a force multiplier. Your data might live in an Azure Synapse Analytics data warehouse. Power BI connects to it natively and with high performance. Your final report can be embedded directly into a Microsoft Teams channel, so your team doesn't even have to leave their chat application to see the data. You can export data to Excel with a single click, and the security is all managed through the same Azure Active Directory your company already uses. This integration removes friction at every step.

Finally, the 2025-2026 roadmap is all about Generative AI with "Copilot." This is a game-changer for accessibility. A manager who doesn't know how to write code can now simply ask a question in plain English (natural language querying), and Copilot will build the report for them. For advanced analysts, Copilot acts as an assistant. Instead of struggling with a complex DAX (Data Analysis Expressions) formula, the analyst can describe the metric they need (e.g., "Give me the year-over-year sales growth for the same period last year"), and Copilot will generate the code. This radically speeds up development and lowers the barrier to entry, which is a key part of the enterprise advantage.

This combination of low cost, deep integration, and powerful AI assistance makes Power BI a dominant force, solidifying its place as a top-demand skill for virtually any data analyst or BI role in a large corporation.

9.2 Advanced Data Visualization with Tableau

If Power BI is the pragmatic, all-in-one solution for the enterprise, Tableau (now owned by Salesforce) is the artist's canvas. It is the other dominant leader in the BI market, and it built its reputation on one thing: unmatched data visualization power. Tableau is renowned for its fluid, flexible interface that empowers analysts to "think visually" and explore data in ways that often lead to deeper, more surprising insights.

The core of working in Tableau revolves around understanding the difference between Dimensions and Measures.

Dimensions are your categorical, qualitative data. Think of them as the "buckets" you use to slice your data. Examples include 'Region', 'Customer Name', 'Product Category', or 'Date'.

Measures are your numerical, quantitative data. These are the numbers you want to aggregate. Examples include 'Sales', 'Profit', 'Quantity', or 'Page Views'.

Tableau's interface is brilliant because it physically separates these in your data pane, encouraging you to drag-and-drop Dimensions to create rows or columns (headers) and Measures to create axes (charts). This simple paradigm is the foundation for all its complex visual power.

A key strength emphasized in this module is Tableau's ability to connect to and blend disparate data sources. While Power BI's data modeling is very structured, Tableau's data blending is often seen as more flexible for on-the-fly analysis. It allows an analyst to pull in a primary data source (like a SQL database) and then "blend" it with a secondary source (like a Google Sheet) on a common field, all within a single worksheet, without having to build a complex, unified model beforehand.

The "Updated Application" for this module demonstrates Tableau's true analytical power. A student is first asked to create a "calculated field." This is more than just a simple chart; it's the creation of new knowledge. For example, they might write the formula SUM([Sales]) / SUM([Profit]) to create a new metric called "Sales-to-Profit Ratio." They can then visualize this new metric just like any other field.

Next, they create a "parameter." This is what makes a dashboard truly interactive and exploratory. A parameter is a dynamic, user-controlled variable. For instance, an analyst could create a parameter called "Choose Metric" with a list of options: 'Sales', 'Profit', 'Quantity'. They then link this parameter to a chart. Now, the end-user has a dropdown menu on their dashboard. When they select 'Sales', the chart shows sales by region. When they select 'Profit', the same chart instantly updates to show profit by region. This transforms the dashboard from a static report into an analytical application.

Real-Time Case Study: The Tableau 2025-2026 Advantage

This leads to the case study: why would a data-driven, analyst-centric company—like a tech startup, a media agency, or a consulting firm—choose Tableau, even with its higher price tag?

The first advantage is unmatched artistic control and visual sophistication. Analysts who "live" in the data often prefer Tableau because it doesn't get in their way. It allows for pixel-perfect control over every element on the dashboard—the fonts, the colors, the layout, the tooltips. This isn't just about making things "pretty"; it's about the ability to design a visual story that guides the user's eye to the most important insight. For consulting firms delivering insights to clients or media companies publishing data journalism, this level of polish is non-negotiable.

The second advantage is its superior ability to connect and blend complex data. In fast-moving tech or media companies, data isn't always in a clean, centralized warehouse. An analyst might need to blend data from a production database, a third-party marketing API, and a local CSV file, all for one analysis. Tableau's flexibility in this area is a significant draw for roles where data is messy and speed-to-insight is critical.

Looking at the 2025-2026 roadmap, Tableau's Generative AI feature is "Tableau Pulse." While it also has natural language querying, its key differentiator is its focus on autonomous data monitoring. Pulse is designed to automatically surface insights and "what's new" in your data for you. It can proactively monitor key metrics and send you alerts in Slack or email (e.g., "Sales in the 'Technology' category have declined 15% this week, driven by the 'West' region"). This shifts the paradigm from "I go to the dashboard to find insights" to "the insights find me."

This is why proficiency in Tableau is a prized job skill. It signals more than just technical ability; it signals a depth of analytical thinking and a talent for "telling a story" visually, which is a critical skill for any dedicated data visualization or business analyst role.

9.3 Dashboard Design and Real-Time Analytics

Knowing how to use Power BI or Tableau is only half the battle. A tool is useless, or even dangerous, if the dashboard it produces is confusing, misleading, or ignored. This module moves beyond the specific tools to focus on the principles of effective dashboard design. The single most important principle is audience analysis. A dashboard is not a one-size-fits-all product. The design must be dictated by who will be using it and what decisions they need to make.

We can break dashboards down into three primary categories:

Strategic Dashboards: These are for the C-suite and executives. The focus is high-level, long-term, and summary-based. An executive doesn't need to see sales by the hour. They need to see high-level Key Performance Indicators (KPIs) like 'Monthly Recurring Revenue', 'Customer Acquisition Cost', and 'Market Share'. The data is often updated daily or weekly, not in real-time. The design is clean, simple, and shows progress against long-term goals.

Analytical Dashboards: These are for data analysts and business analysts. Unlike strategic dashboards, these are not for at-a-glance monitoring. They are for exploration. These dashboards are packed with filters, parameters, and drill-down capabilities. The goal is to allow the analyst to "live in the data," ask new questions, and uncover the "why" behind the numbers. This is where you'd use Tableau's parameters or Power BI's drill-through features.

Operational Dashboards: These are for front-line managers and operational teams (e.g., a logistics manager, a call center supervisor, a factory floor manager). The focus is on real-time monitoring and alerts. The data must be as close to "now" as possible. The goal is to spot problems and opportunities as they happen and take immediate action.

The key design principle for all dashboards, but especially operational ones, is minimizing "time-to-insight." This is the measure of how quickly a user can look at the dashboard and get the piece of information they need to make a decision. A good dashboard has a clear visual hierarchy. The most critical KPI (e.g., "Systems Down" or "Packages Delayed") should be in the top-left corner, in a large font, and use color (like red) to draw the eye immediately. A bad dashboard is a cluttered collection of 20 different charts, forcing the user to hunt for the one number that matters.

The "Updated Application" for this module is a perfect practical test. A student is given the persona of a "logistics manager" and tasked with designing an operational dashboard. Their first job isn't to open the BI tool; it's to define the KPIs. What does this manager need to know right now? They'd select KPIs like:

'Trucks On-Time vs. Delayed' (as a percentage)

'Average Unload Time' (in minutes)

'Real-Time Location' (on a map)

'Critical Alerts' (e.g., "Vehicle 104: High Engine Temp")

The design would place the alerts and the "Delayed" percentage front-and-center, using the map as a secondary reference. This design is focused purely on enabling real-time action.

Real-Time Case Study: Geotab's Fleet Management

There is no better example of a high-stakes, real-time operational dashboard than Geotab. Geotab is a global leader in telematics and fleet management. They process billions of data points per day from over 4.6 million connected vehicles. Their customers are fleet managers who need to know precisely what is happening with their assets right now.

Geotab's dashboards are a masterclass in operational design. They provide fleet managers with:

Real-Time Route Optimization: A manager can see a live map of all their vehicles and compare their current routes against a planned route. If a truck is stuck in traffic, the system can send an alert to reroute them.

Driver Safety Alerts: The telematics device in the truck monitors behavior like harsh braking, speeding, and seatbelt use. A "Watchdog Report" or a live safety scorecard on the dashboard can show the manager which drivers are creating risk, allowing for immediate coaching.

Maintenance & Decarbonization: The dashboard monitors engine health, fault codes, and, critically, idle time. A manager can see a report of all trucks that idled for more than 30 minutes that day, a massive source of wasted fuel and carbon emissions. This dashboard directly enables action (e.g., "Call the driver of Truck 108 and ask why they've been idling for 45 minutes").

This case study demonstrates that a well-designed operational dashboard isn't just a report; it's an active part of the business operation. This is why the Job Skill Enhancement is "Dashboard & Report Creation." It's not just a technical skill; it's a business skill that requires you to combine your knowledge of the tool (Tableau or Power BI) with a deep understanding of what the end-user actually needs to do their job.

9.4 Enterprise BI Platform Comparison (2025-2026)

This module brings everything together into a direct, head-to-head comparison of the two market leaders, Power BI and Tableau. Understanding the business and technical trade-offs between these platforms is a crucial skill for any analyst or manager. Based on 2025-2026 market analysis, here is the executive summary of the "BI wars."

Market Share: As of 2025, the market is incredibly tight, but Power BI has taken a slight lead in overall market share, hovering around 13.9% compared to Tableau's 13.0%. This is a recent development and shows Power BI's aggressive growth, largely fueled by its pricing and ecosystem advantages.

Cost: This is the clearest point of difference. Power BI is the undisputed winner on affordability. As mentioned, its "Pro" license is a low monthly per-user fee, and it's often bundled into existing Microsoft 365 E5 enterprise agreements. Tableau, by contrast, is known to be "aggressively expensive." Its licensing model is also per-user but at a much higher price point, which can become a significant barrier to scaling BI across an entire organization.

Ease of Use: This is a nuanced debate. Power BI is generally considered easier for beginners, especially those who come from a heavy Excel background. The interface, the Power Query editor, and the DAX formula language are all conceptually similar to advanced Excel features like PivotTables and Power Pivot. Tableau is often considered more intuitive for experienced data analysts and those who "think visually." Its drag-and-drop, canvas-like feel is often preferred by analysts who want to explore data without first having to build a rigid data model.

AI Integration (2025-2026): Both platforms have strong, competing Generative AI roadmaps. Power BI has "Copilot," which is deeply integrated into the Microsoft ecosystem. Its strengths are in-report generation (e.g., "create a bar chart of sales by region") and, most importantly, DAX generation to help analysts write complex code. Tableau has "Tableau Pulse," which is more focused on proactive, autonomous insights. Its strength is in automatically monitoring metrics, identifying significant changes, and alerting users in their workflow (like Slack) before they even open a dashboard.

The "Updated Application" for this module is a decision-making framework. If you are a student or analyst looking to learn a new skill, the guidance is: "Learn Power BI if you are targeting large, established corporations, especially in finance, healthcare, or retail, as they are likely Microsoft shops. Learn Tableau if you are targeting tech, media, or consulting, where its advanced visualization and exploratory power are highly valued."

If you are a manager deciding which tool to purchase, the framework is: "Choose Power BI if your company is already in the Microsoft ecosystem (using Azure, M365) and your primary goal is to democratize data and provide a 'good enough' BI solution to the largest number of users at the lowest cost. Choose Tableau if your primary need is for a dedicated team of analysts to perform deep, complex visual exploration, and you have the budget to support it."

Real-Time Case Study: The Business Case: Why Power BI is Winning

This 2025-era case study analyzes the business-level decision-making that explains Power BI's rapid rise in market share. It frames the debate in a way that is very familiar to any IT or finance leader.

While a survey of data analysts might show a preference for Tableau's advanced features and visual flexibility, the person signing the check—the CFO or CIO—sees a different picture. From their perspective, Tableau is "aggressively expensive." A large-scale, enterprise-wide deployment can cost hundreds of thousands, or even millions, of dollars more than a comparable Power BI rollout.

Management then asks a simple question: "Is Tableau that much better?" For most common business use cases—a sales dashboard, a financial report, an operational KPI tracker—the answer is "no." Power BI is seen as "at least an adequate alternative" that gets the job done at a fraction of the cost.

This cost-benefit analysis makes the business case for Power BI incredibly compelling. The ability to give 10,000 employees a BI tool for the same price as giving 1,000 employees Tableau is a simple, powerful value proposition. This explains why Power BI is "winning" in terms of new enterprise adoption.

This leads to the final Job Skill Enhancement: Tool Selection & Market Awareness. As a data professional, you are more valuable if you are not just a "Tableau person" or a "Power BI person." You are most valuable when you can understand the business context—the budget, the existing tech stack, the user's goals—and recommend the right tool for the job. This market awareness is what separates a good analyst from a great strategic partner.

Data Governance, Quality, and Ethical Practice

Subtopic 10.1: Principles of Modern Data Governance

Data governance is one of the most misunderstood and, frankly, poorly implemented disciplines in the modern organization. For years, it was relegated to a back-office IT function, seen as a compliance-driven cost center that just slowed things down. It was a binder of rules on a shelf. That era is definitively over.

Today, and especially as we move through 2025, data governance is a core business strategy. It is the formal, active, and executive-led establishment of policies, roles, and standards to manage and safeguard an organization's data as its most critical strategic asset. It is the source code for building trust in your data. Without it, you don't have a "data lake"; you have a "data swamp"—a murky, unreliable, and dangerous place to build a business.

At its heart, governance is built on four essential pillars. Lose one, and the entire structure becomes unstable.

Data Quality: This is the most visible pillar. It ensures data is accurate, complete, consistent, and timely. It's the commitment that the number in your report is the right number, and that everyone in the company agrees on it.

Data Management: This pillar covers the full lifecycle of data, from its creation and storage to its archival and eventual deletion. It includes data architecture, database operations, and performance.

Data Security: This is a distinct and critical function. It's not just about managing the data but protecting it. This pillar defines who can access what data, when, and under what circumstances. It includes encryption, access controls, and threat monitoring.

Compliance: This pillar enforces the external rules of the road. It ensures all data handling practices adhere to legal and regulatory standards like GDPR, CCPA, and industry-specific rules (like HIPAA in healthcare).

To make these pillars operational, you need people. The most common failure I've seen in the field is when organizations buy an expensive governance tool but fail to define human accountability. Two roles are non-negotiable: the Data Owner and the Data Steward.

The Data Owner is a senior business-side leader. The VP of Sales, for example, is the Data Owner for all sales data (like customer accounts and leads). This person is accountable for the quality, security, and ethical use of that data. They don't do the technical work, but they set the rules (e.g., "Only the sales team and finance can see a customer's contract details").

The Data Steward is the responsible party, often closer to the data itself—perhaps a senior IT professional or a lead business analyst. This person is responsible for implementing the Owner's rules. They manage data definitions, monitor data quality, and are the day-to-day contacts for that specific data domain. They are the guardians at the gate.

The entire system is held together by active metadata management. Metadata, or "data about data," is the foundation for scalable governance. In the past, this was a static "data dictionary" in an Excel file that was obsolete the moment it was saved. Today, active metadata is dynamic. It's a living system that tracks data lineage (Where did this number come from?), usage (Who is using this report?), and quality, often automatically.

A practical application of this is building a "data compliance framework" for a new project. This begins with a Data Dictionary, a core form of metadata. It's not just a list of technical field names. It's a business contract.

Field Name

Data Type

Definition

Governance Rules

cust_email

VARCHAR(255)

The primary email address for user login and communication.

PII - Encrypted at Rest - Access restricted to HR & Auth Services.

last_order_date

TIMESTAMP

The timestamp of the user's most recent completed purchase.

Business Data - Not PII - Access for Marketing, Sales, Analytics.

ssn

CHAR(9)

Social Security Number for U.S. employees.

SPI (Sensitive PII) - Encrypted & Masked - Access restricted to Payroll (last 4 digits only).

This simple chart is the start of real governance. It forces a conversation before data is ever collected.

The real-world case study of JPMorgan Chase's (JPMC) "Data Mesh" shows what this looks like at massive scale. For decades, the standard model was a single, central data warehouse team. This created a monumental bottleneck. Every business unit had to get in line to ask the central team for data, and that team became overwhelmed, unable to understand the business context for thousands of requests.

JPMC's "data mesh" architecture flips this model. It's a decentralized approach built on a common governance framework. The core idea is "data as a product." The "Consumer Banking" domain, for instance, owns its data. It is responsible for cleaning, securing, and serving that data as a finished "product" to the rest of the firm via standard, secure APIs. The central data team evolves from being a gatekeeper to an enabler—they build the "roads" (the common platform and governance rules), and the business domains build their "factories" on that infrastructure. This model dramatically improved data tracking, auditing, and governance, allowing a massive institution to move faster and more safely.

This is why Data Governance is a critical job skill. As companies mature and, most importantly, as they rush to feed their data into AI models, robust governance is the non-negotiable prerequisite. It's the business necessity that ensures you're building your future on a foundation of stone, not sand.

Subtopic 10.2: Data Quality Management and MDM

If data governance is the strategic framework, Data Quality (DQ) management is where the rubber meets the road. It is the tactical, ongoing process of ensuring that an organization's data is fit for its intended purpose. Every analyst has felt the pain of "bad data." In my experience, most analysts spend up to 80% of their time just cleaning and preparing data, and only 20% on actual analysis. This is a massive, soul-crushing waste of talent and resources.

The goal is to evolve from this ad-hoc, reactive data cleaning to a systematic, proactive Data Quality (DQ) framework.

The "ad-hoc" method, as taught in introductory analytics, is what you do to a single, static file. You get a messy CSV, so you open a Python script, remove null values, standardize date formats, and fix typos. The problem is solved... for that one file, on that one day. When the next data pull happens, all the same problems reappear because the root cause was never fixed.

A systematic DQ framework moves the solution "upstream." Instead of cleaning the data after it lands in the analyst's lap, it sets policies and uses analytics tools to monitor and fix data at its source. This is a profound shift from data janitor to data manager.

The most effective way to do this is through automated, rule-based alerts. This is an "Updated Application" of analytics tools. You are, in effect, using analytics to analyze your own data processes. These aren't complex models; they are simple, powerful business rules that act as an early warning system.

Example 1: The "Negative Price" Alert. A rule is set: flag any new order in the 'orders' table where 'price' < 0. This alert is routed immediately to the Data Steward for the e-commerce platform. They can investigate: Is it a data entry typo? Is it a bug in the checkout system processing a refund incorrectly? Is it fraud? The problem is caught in minutes, not weeks later by an analyst.

Example 2: The "Volume Drop" Alert. A rule is set: alert if 'daily_user_signups' is 20% below the 30-day moving average. This alert goes to the Marketing Data Steward. They can check: Did a marketing campaign just end? Or did the website's signup form break?

Example 3: The "Inconsistent State" Alert. A rule is set: flag any new record in the 'customer' table where the 'state' field is not a 2-letter abbreviation. This prevents "CA," "Calif.," and "California" from all co-existing.

This framework is essential, but it often only addresses new data. What about the decades of conflicting, duplicated data already sitting in your systems? This is the problem solved by Master Data Management (MDM).

MDM is the technology and discipline for creating and maintaining a "single source of truth" for an organization's most critical, shared data assets. These aren't transaction-level data (like an individual web click) but master data—the core nouns of the business. The most common MDM domains are:

Customer: Who are our customers?

Product: What do we sell?

Supplier: Who do we buy from?

Location: Where are our assets?

The "single source of truth" problem is universal. I've worked with a Fortune 500 company where the Sales team's "customer list" (in Salesforce) had 1.2 million records. The Marketing team's list (in their email tool) had 1.8 million. And the Finance team's billing system had 900,000. So, how many customers do they have? The answer was, "it depends on who you ask." This is a business-crippling problem. A customer updates their address with a sales rep, but the finance department keeps sending invoices to the old address.

An MDM platform solves this. It sits in the center, connects to all these systems, and ingests their data. It then uses sophisticated matching, merging, and de-duplication rules to identify that "John Smith," "J. Smith," and "John A. Smith" at the same address are all the same person. It creates a single "golden record" for that customer. This master record becomes the single source of truth, and updates are then pushed back to the connected systems, ensuring everyone is working from the same, trusted data.

The "Walmart's Supply Chain Optimization" case study is a classic, powerful example of MDM in action. Walmart's business is built on logistical excellence. But with tens of thousands of suppliers and millions of products, that excellence is impossible if the data is messy. If one supplier calls a product Widget-A-Blue and another calls it Blue Widget (Model A), a simple query for "how many blue widgets do we have in stock?" becomes impossible.

By implementing data governance and MDM, Walmart created a single source of truth for its "Supplier" and "Product" master data. Every supplier was given a single ID. Every product was standardized into a single catalog. This wasn't just a data-cleaning project; it was a fundamental business transformation. It allowed Walmart to reduce stockouts (because they knew what they had), dramatically improve inventory forecasting (because they could analyze sales for a single product, not 50 variations of it), and enhance operational efficiency across their entire global network.

This is why Data Quality Management is such a vital skill. It builds trust. If your stakeholders and executives do not trust the data, they will not trust your analysis. Period. An analyst who can move beyond simply using data to actively improving it becomes an invaluable asset and a true partner to the business.

Subtopic 10.3: Data Privacy, Security, and Compliance (2025)

This module moves from "good practice" to "non-negotiable mandate." In 2025, data privacy, security, and compliance are no longer IT-centric issues; they are board-level, existential risks. A failure in this domain can result in massive financial penalties, crippling legal consequences, and a catastrophic, often permanent, loss of customer trust. For any data analyst, understanding these rules is as fundamental as understanding SQL.

The core of modern compliance is driven by a new generation of global regulations. The two most significant are:

GDPR (General Data Protection Regulation): This is the European Union's landmark law, and it has become the de facto global standard. It mandates strict, clear guidelines on how any organization, anywhere in the world, must handle the data of EU citizens. Its core principles include the "right to be forgotten" (a user can demand data deletion), "data portability" (a user can request a copy of their data), and, most importantly, "lawful basis for processing." You cannot simply collect data "just in case." You must have a specific, documented, and legal reason for every single piece of personal data you store.

CCPA/CPRA (California Consumer Privacy Act / Privacy Rights Act): This is California's version, granting similar rights to its residents, including the right to opt out of their data being sold. The key takeaway is that this is the direction of all future regulation. What happens in the EU and California quickly spreads.

To meet these requirements, analysts and engineers must employ privacy-preserving techniques. This isn't just a setting you "turn on"; it's a multi-layered design philosophy.

Encryption: This is the most basic technical control. It means scrambling data so it's unreadable without a specific "key." This must be done for data at rest (sitting in a database) and data in transit (moving over a network).

Data Minimization: This is a powerful, non-technical concept mandated by the GDPR. It is the simple principle of collecting only what is absolutely necessary. The old mindset was "collect everything; we'll find a use for it later." The 2025 mindset is "If I don't need your date of birth to send you a newsletter, I will not ask for it." The safest way to handle sensitive data is to not have it in the first place.

Data Anonymization/Pseudonymization: This is crucial for analysts. Anonymization involves permanently breaking the link between data and an individual (e.g., user_123 becomes random_hash_ABC, and the key is destroyed). Pseudonymization involves replacing PII with a token, where the link is stored, but in a separate, highly secure system. Analysts can work with the pseudonymized data for trends, while only a few privileged applications (like billing) can re-identify the user.

A key 2025-specific trend in this area is the increased focus on protecting teen data. Regulators and the public have recognized that minors are a uniquely vulnerable population. This has led to new laws demanding much stricter, age-verified parental consent for data collection, outright bans on targeted advertising to teens, and requirements for all settings to be "private-by-default." For any company in social media, gaming, or educational technology, this is a primary compliance and ethical challenge.

The "Updated Application" for this module is the "privacy-by-design" audit. This is a core practice that embeds privacy into a project from its very first day, rather than trying to "bolt it on" at the end. Before launching a new analytics project, a student learns to perform this audit:

Identify PII: What Personal Identifiable Information (PII) will this project touch? (e.g., name, email, IP address, geolocation).

Define Legal Basis: What is our legal right to use this data? (e.g., explicit user consent, to fulfill a contract).

Ensure Security: How will this data be secured? (e.g., encrypted at rest, access restricted to three specific analysts).

Define Retention: What is our data retention policy? (e.g., "We will delete the raw geolocation data after 90 days and only store the aggregated, anonymized results").

This audit, performed before a project launches, is the single best way to prevent a privacy disaster.

The "Snowflake Breach (2024-2025)" serves as a chilling, real-time case study of what happens when these principles are ignored. Snowflake is a leading data platform, but many of its customers were breached in 2024 and 2025. The attackers (reportedly) didn't exploit a flaw in Snowflake's core technology. Instead, they exploited a massive data governance failure on the part of the customers.

Attackers used credentials stolen from other breaches (like old passwords from other websites) and found they worked on customer Snowflake accounts. The critical lesson was that the breached customers had failed to implement basic, pillar-level safeguards:

They had not enforced multi-factor authentication (MFA).

They had given users (and service accounts) far too broad access privileges.

They were not performing continuous monitoring or activity logging to detect suspicious behavior (like a massive data download from an unrecognized IP address).

This breach is a stark reminder that the most advanced technology in the world is useless if your data governance and security practices are weak. Data privacy and compliance are mandatory, non-negotiable skills for any analyst in 2025. A single mistake—like exporting a customer list to an unsecured laptop or emailing an unencrypted file—is no longer just a "mistake." It is a breach that can cost millions of dollars, invite legal action, and permanently destroy the trust you and your company have worked for years to build.

Subtopic 10.4: Data Ethics and AI Governance

This final subtopic transcends the others. It moves beyond what is profitable (Subtopic 10.1), what is correct (Subtopic 10.2), and what is legal (Subtopic 10.3). This is about what is right. As data professionals, we are building the systems that decide who gets a loan, who gets a job interview, and what information people see. This power comes with a profound, non-negotiable ethical responsibility.

Compliance is the floor; ethics is the ceiling. A decision can be perfectly legal but still be ethically wrong, unfair, or harmful. This is the complex gray area where true data leaders are forged.

The most pervasive ethical challenge is Data Bias. An AI model is not objective. It is a mirror that reflects the data it was trained on, including all of that data's historical, systemic, and human biases. The model doesn't "learn" to be fair; it learns to be statistically accurate based on the past. If the past was biased, the AI will not only perpetuate that bias, it will amplify and automate it at scale.

Example: Hiring Bias. Imagine you train an AI model to screen resumes for a software engineer role. You feed it 20 years of your company's hiring data. If, in that 20-year history, the company predominantly hired men for that role, the AI will learn that "being male" is a strong predictor of "being hired." It will then start to penalize resumes from qualified women, even if gender is not explicitly listed as a feature. It might learn to penalize "all-women's college" or "women's software club." The AI isn't "sexist"; it is simply, and dangerously, matching the patterns in biased data.

Example: Lending Bias. A model trained on historical mortgage data might learn that applicants from certain zip codes (which often correlate with race) are less likely to repay loans. The model's "denial" is not based on the individual's creditworthiness but on a biased proxy for it. The outcome is discriminatory.

This leads to the critical issues of Fairness & Accountability. If an AI model, acting as a "black box," denies someone a critical opportunity, who is responsible? When the person asks "why?", the answer "because the algorithm said so" is unacceptable. Is it the data scientist who built the model? The data owner who supplied the biased data? The executive who approved its use without proper testing? This lack of accountability is a central ethical crisis.

The 2025-centric field of AI Governance emerges as the solution. This is an extension of data governance, but specifically for AI models and systems. It is a framework for monitoring AI for ethics, bias, risk, and explainability. It is a C-suite-level function designed to manage the entire lifecycle of a model, from conception to retirement. It involves constantly asking: Is the model's accuracy drifting? Is it exhibiting biased outcomes against any protected group? Can we explain, in simple terms, why it made a particular decision?

The "Updated Application" for this module is learning to audit an algorithm for bias. This is a practical skill for all modern analysts.

The Scenario: A bank builds a simple credit-scoring model.

The Audit: An analyst doesn't just check the model's overall accuracy. They segment its performance. They run the model on a test group of 1,000 applicants (where the "correct" outcome is known).

The Finding: The analyst finds the model is 95% accurate for applicants from Zip Code A, but only 65% accurate for applicants from Zip Code B. Even worse, its "false negative" rate (unfairly denying qualified applicants) is 10 times higher for Zip Code B.

The Mitigation: The analyst has proven the model is biased. The solution is not to "tweak the code." It requires a fundamental intervention, such as re-sampling the training data to get more examples from under-represented groups, or even adding a mathematical "fairness constraint" to the model itself.

The "AI Chatbot Failures (2025)" case study is a terrifying, real-world example of what happens when AI governance fails completely. We have seen multiple, stark reports in 2025 where AI-powered chatbots, due to poor design and a total lack of ethical guardrails, "urged minors to engage in self-harm, suicide and violence against parents."

This is not a theoretical risk. It is a real, documented harm. It represents a catastrophic breakdown at every level of governance:

Failed Design: The models were not designed with "safety" as their primary objective.

Failed Testing: The systems were clearly not tested for these "adversarial" or sensitive edge cases.

Failed Guardrails: There were no rules to immediately stop the AI from discussing self-harm or violence.

Failed Monitoring: There was no system in place to flag this behavior and shut it down.

This case study is a visceral lesson in the severe, human consequences of failed AI governance. This is why "Data Ethics & AI Governance" is the critical skill that separates a "technician" from a "strategic, responsible leader." A technician can build an AI model. A leader asks should we build this model, and if so, how do we build it safely and fairly? As AI becomes exponentially more powerful, the professionals who can navigate these ethical waters and govern this technology responsibly are becoming the most invaluable people in any organization.

PART IV: ADVANCED MODELING AND SPECIALIZATIONS

Applied Supervised Machine Learning for Analytics

11.1: Foundations of Supervised Learning: Classification vs. Regression

Welcome to the foundational concepts of supervised machine learning. If you're new to this field, the easiest way to think about it is as a specialized form of teaching. Imagine you're trying to teach a computer to identify things, not with abstract rules, but with concrete examples. This "teaching by example" is the entire essence of supervised learning.

The "supervisor" in this process isn't a person, but rather the labeled data we provide. This is the core concept. Labeled data is simply a dataset where the "answer" is already known. We don't just give the computer a list of house specifications; we give it a list of house specifications and the price each house actually sold for. That "sold price" is the label. We don't just show it a customer's activity; we show it the customer's activity and a label "Yes" or "No" for whether they actually churned. The model "learns" by trying to find the mathematical patterns that connect the features (the house specs, the customer activity) to the known label (the answer).

Once the model has "learned" these patterns from thousands or even millions of examples, its real value emerges: we can now give it new, unlabeled data—a brand new house listing, a current customer—and ask it to predict the answer.

In the world of business analytics, this powerful tool is primarily split into two fundamental tasks. This split isn't academic; it's the first question you must answer before you write a single line of code. Everything about your project—your model choice, your success metrics, and your final deliverable—depends on it. These two tasks are Regression and Classification.

📈 Regression: Predicting a Number

A regression task is any problem where you are trying to predict a continuous, numerical value. The "answer" you're seeking can exist on a spectrum. Think of it as a "How much?" or "How many?" problem.

The classic example is predicting a house price, like "$350,000." But the business applications are endless, and they are often the most high-value questions a company can ask:

Finance: "What will the projected revenue be for the next quarter?" (Predicting a specific dollar amount).

Marketing: "How much will this specific new customer spend in their first year?" (This is called Customer Lifetime Value, or LTV, prediction).

Operations: "How many minutes will this support call last?" (Used for resource planning).

E-commerce: "How many units of this blue sweater will we sell in our Texas warehouses next week?" (This is demand forecasting, a critical regression problem).

In each case, the output isn't a simple category; it's a number. When a regression model is wrong, its error is also numerical. It didn't predict "Blue" when the answer was "Red"; it predicted "$340,000" when the answer was "$350,000," an error of $10,000.

Classification: Predicting a Category

A classification task, on the other hand, is any problem where you are trying to predict a categorical, discrete outcome. The "answer" belongs to a specific, predefined "class" or "bucket." Think of this as a "Which one?" or "Will it?" problem.

Classification problems are arguably the most common in business analytics. They are further divided into two types:

Binary Classification: This is the most common of all. The "answer" has only two possible outcomes, usually a "Yes" or "No" question.

"Will this customer churn or not churn?"

"Is this transaction fraudulent or not fraudulent?"

"Will this marketing lead convert or not convert?"

"Is this email spam or not spam?"

Multi-Class Classification: This is when the "answer" has three or more possible categories, but it's still a single choice.

"Is this customer support ticket about 'Billing', 'Technical', or 'Sales'?"

"Which news category does this article belong to: 'Sports', 'Politics', or 'Technology'?"

"What is the sentiment of this customer review: 'Positive', 'Negative', or 'Neutral'?"

Framing: The Most Critical Skill

This brings us to the Real-Time Case Study: "Framing the Telco Churn Problem." In this dataset, we have thousands of records of past customers. We have their "features" (tenure, monthly charges, contract type) and, critically, we have the "label"—a column named Churn that contains either "Yes" or "No."

Because the goal is to predict an outcome from a predefined category ("Yes" or "No"), this is a classic supervised classification problem. We are "supervising" the model by showing it thousands of examples of what "Yes" customers and "No" customers look like.

This "framing" step is a critical skill for any analyst. A stakeholder might come to you with a vague request like, "I want to know about customer risk." This is not an ML problem; it's a business idea. It's your job to frame it.

Bad Frame: "Predict customer risk." (What does this mean?)

Regression Frame: "Predict the dollar amount a customer will default on in the next 12 months." (Goal: a number, e.g., "$500").

Classification Frame: "Predict if a customer will default on any payment in the next 12 months." (Goal: a category, e.g., "Yes" or "No").

Both are valid, but they solve different business problems and require different models. Getting this first step wrong means you could build a perfectly accurate model that solves a problem nobody has. Understanding this distinction isn't just "Machine Learning Basics"; it's the entire foundation of predictive analytics in a business context.

11.2: Logistic Regression and K-Nearest Neighbors (kNN)

Once you have correctly framed your business problem as a supervised classification task—for example, "Will this customer churn?"—the next step is to actually build a model. In the vast toolkit of machine learning, there are two algorithms that stand as the most foundational and essential starting points: Logistic Regression and K-Nearest Neighbors (kNN).

These models are your "classics." They are taught in every introductory course and used in every data science team for a simple reason: they are fast, easy to understand, and incredibly useful. More importantly, they provide the "baseline" against which all other, more complex models must be judged.

Logistic Regression: The Interpretable Baseline

Despite its name, Logistic Regression is a classification algorithm, not a regression one. It's the go-to model for solving binary (Yes/No) problems.

Its core idea is to adapt Linear Regression (which predicts numbers by fitting a straight line) for classification. Here's how it works:

It starts by creating a linear equation, just like linear regression, that combines all the features (e.g., score=w1 ·tenure+w2·monthly_charges+...).

The "magic" happens next. It takes this raw score (which could be any number, like -10 or 50) and passes it through a special function called the sigmoid function.

This S-shaped function squishes any number it receives into a value between 0 and 1.

A Logistic Regression model doesn't just say "Churn." It says, "Based on this customer's data, there is a 75% probability that they will churn." This is vastly more useful to a business. You can now create a "risk list" and prioritize your retention efforts, starting with the customers who have a 95% churn probability, then 90%, and so on.

Its other key advantage is interpretability. Because it's a statistical model, you can look "under the hood" at its coefficients (w1, w2, etc.) and understand why it's making its predictions. You can state with statistical confidence, "For every additional month a customer's tenure increases, the odds of them churning decrease by 5%." This kind of insight is pure gold for business leaders.

🏘 K-Nearest Neighbors (kNN): The "Intuitive" Classifier

K-Nearest Neighbors (kNN) is completely different. It's not a statistical model; it's an "instance-based" or "lazy-learning" model. It has one of the simplest, most intuitive concepts in all of machine learning:

"You are classified by the company you keep."

kNN works by assuming that similar things exist in close proximity. To classify a new data point (a new customer), it simply "plots" them in a multi-dimensional space with all the old data points (your entire training set).

Then, it looks at the "k" closest neighbors to that new point. The value of 'k' is something you decide (e.g., k=5, k=10).

If you set k=5, the model finds the 5 absolute closest data points from the training data.

It then takes a "vote." If 3 of those 5 neighbors are "Churn=Yes" and 2 are "Churn=No," the model predicts "Churn=Yes" for the new customer.

This is a "lazy" algorithm because there is no real "training" phase. It "learns" by simply memorizing the entire dataset. All the hard work and computation happen at prediction time, when it has to calculate the "distance" from the new point to every single other point in the dataset.

The main downsides of kNN are that it can be very slow on large datasets (imagine calculating 1 million "distances" for every new prediction) and it's sensitive to the scale of your features. A "Salary" feature (e.g., 50,000) will have a much larger impact on the "distance" calculation than an "Age" feature (e.g., 40), so all data must be scaled (e.g., put on a 0-1 scale) before using kNN.

The Real-World Application: "The Baseline Churn Model"

This brings us to the Real-Time Case Study: "The Baseline Churn Model." This is a critical workflow that separates amateur analysts from professionals.

No experienced data scientist jumps straight to a complex, "fancy" algorithm. Their first step is always to build a baseline model. Logistic Regression is the perfect tool for this.

Why? Because it's fast to build and easy to interpret. You run it on your churn dataset, and it gives you a performance score, for example, "78% accuracy."

This 78% is now your benchmark. It's the "score to beat."

This baseline is your anchor. It answers the most important question: "Is this new, complex model actually better?"

If you build a simple kNN model and it gets 76% accuracy, you know it's worse than your simple baseline.

If you spend two weeks building a highly complex "deep learning" neural network and it gets 78.2% accuracy, you have a serious problem. You can't justify the extra complexity, cost, and maintenance for a tiny 0.2% gain. The baseline model is superior.

But, if you build a Random Forest (from the next module) and it gets 82% accuracy, you can now prove its value. You can go to your manager and say, "The baseline model was 78% accurate, but my new model is 82% accurate. This 4% lift translates to correctly identifying 5,000 more at-risk customers per quarter."

Building classification models in tools like Scikit-learn is a core job skill. But knowing how to use them to establish a baseline and compare them using metrics like accuracy, precision, and recall is what makes you a valuable analyst.

11.3: Tree-Based Models: Decision Trees and Random Forests

After establishing a baseline with a model like Logistic Regression, the next logical step for an analyst is to explore models that can capture more complex, non-linear relationships in the data. This is where tree-based models shine. They are, without question, some of the most popular, powerful, and (in their basic form) interpretable models in the machine learning world.

This family of models starts with a simple, intuitive concept—the Decision Tree—and evolves into one of the most robust and high-performing "workhorse" algorithms available: the Random Forest.

🌳 Decision Trees: The Flowchart Model

A Decision Tree is exactly what it sounds like. It's a model that makes predictions by following a flowchart of "if-then" questions. It's perhaps the most human-understandable algorithm because it mimics how we often make decisions in real life.

Here's how it learns:

It starts with the entire dataset (the "root node").

It searches through every feature (Tenure, Contract, Monthly Charges) and finds the single best question it can ask that will split the dataset into two "purer" groups—groups that are more "Yes-Churn" or "No-Churn" than the original.

For example, it might find the best question is: "Is Contract = 'Month-to-Month'?"

This splits the data into two branches: a "Yes" branch (all Month-to-Month customers) and a "No" branch (all 1-Year or 2-Year contract customers).

It then repeats this process on each new branch. On the "Yes" branch, it might find the next best question is "Is

Tenure < 12 months?" On the "No" branch, the best question might be "Is Monthly Charges > $100?"

It continues splitting the data, growing "branches" and "leaves" until it reaches a "leaf node"—a final prediction (e.g., "Churn=Yes").

The primary advantage of Decision Trees is their white-box interpretability. You can literally print out the entire tree and show it to a business manager. It's not a black box; it's a set of simple, understandable rules. "If a customer is Month-to-Month and their tenure is less than 12 months, our data shows they have an 88% probability of churning."

However, this simplicity comes with a massive, fatal flaw: overfitting.

If you let a Decision Tree grow to its full depth, it will keep asking questions until it has perfectly sorted every single person in your training data. It will create hyper-specific rules like, "If Contract=M-t-M AND Tenure=5 months AND MonthlyCharge=$72.50... then Churn=Yes." This model will have 100% accuracy on the data it trained on, but it has "memorized" the noise, not the "signal." The moment you show it a new customer, it will fail, because it's never seen that exact combination before.

🌲🌲🌲 Random Forests: The "Wisdom of the Crowd"

How do you fix the overfitting problem of a single, highly-specific Decision Tree? You build hundreds of them and have them vote. This is the core idea of a Random Forest.

A Random Forest is an ensemble method. "Ensemble" is just a fancy word for a model that is made up of many other, simpler models. It leverages the "wisdom of the crowd" principle: a large group of "pretty good" predictors will be much more accurate and stable than a single, "perfect" (but overfit) predictor.

It's not just "building 500 trees." A Random Forest introduces two key "tricks" to ensure the trees are diverse and don't all make the same mistakes. This technique is called bagging (Bootstrap Aggregating):

Random Data (Bootstrapping): Each of the 500 trees is not given the full dataset. Instead, it's given a random sample of the data (drawn "with replacement"). This means each tree "grows up" learning from a slightly different "version" of the data, making it a "specialist" in that particular subset.

Random Features (Feature Subspacing): At each split (each "if-then" question), the tree is not allowed to search through all the features. It's only allowed to pick from a random subset of features (e.g., "At this node, you can only ask a question about 'Tenure', 'Internet Service', or 'Dependents'").

These two tricks create an "ensemble" of 500 de-correlated trees. They are all slightly different, have different "specialties," and will all make different, random errors.

When it's time to make a prediction for a new customer, all 500 trees "vote." If 400 trees vote "Churn" and 100 vote "No Churn," the final prediction is "Churn." The individual errors and "overfitting" of each tree get canceled out by the majority vote, leaving only the strong, true "signal."

Application: Delivering Insights with Feature Importance

Random Forests are robust, high-performing "out-of-the-box" algorithms. But one of their most powerful applications for an analyst is feature importance.

After the model is trained, you can ask it, "Which features did you find most useful for making your predictions?" Because the model built 500 trees, it can look back and see which features were most often used to create good "splits."

It will give you a ranked list:

Contract Type: 35% Importance

Tenure: 28% Importance

Monthly Charges: 16% Importance

Tech Support: 8% Importance

...and so on.

This is a power-packed deliverable. You can go to management and say, "We built an 82% accurate churn model. But more importantly, it told us that Contract Type is the single biggest driver of churn. We need to find a way to move our 'Month-to-Month' customers onto '1-Year' contracts." This is how an analyst delivers actionable insights, not just predictions.

The 2025 "E-commerce Churn Prediction" case study validates this. When compared directly, the Random Forest model outperformed the simple Decision Tree, kNN, and others. The Decision Tree overfit, and the kNN couldn't handle the complex interactions, but the Random Forest's "ensemble" approach provided the best balance of performance and stability. Proficiency with this "workhorse" algorithm is a non-negotiable skill for any analyst moving into predictive roles.

11.4: Advanced Ensemble Models: Gradient Boosting (XGBoost & LightGBM)

If Logistic Regression is your baseline and Random Forest is your reliable "workhorse," then Gradient Boosting Machines (GBM) are your high-performance, precision-tuned supercars. This module introduces the "king" of algorithms for structured, tabular data—the kind of spreadsheet-style data you work with every single day in business.

When you have a high-stakes prediction problem (like churn, fraud, or lead-scoring) and you need the absolute best performance, you turn to Gradient Boosting. This is an advanced ensemble technique that has become the dominant, industry-standard approach. This module focuses on the two libraries that implement this idea: XGBoost (Extreme Gradient Boosting) and LightGBM (Light Gradient Boosting).

The Core Concept: Boosting vs. Bagging

To understand why boosting is so powerful, you must first understand how it's fundamentally different from the Random Forest (which uses "bagging").

Random Forest (Bagging): This is a parallel process. It's like building 500 independent Decision Trees in separate rooms, giving each a random slice of the data, and then having them all "vote" at the end. It's a "democracy" of models.

Gradient Boosting (Boosting): This is a sequential process. It's like building a team of "specialists" one after another. It's a "meritocracy" built on correcting mistakes.

Here is the "lived experience" of how a Gradient Boosting model trains:

Tree 1: The model builds one simple, "weak" tree (e.g., maybe only 8 "leaves"). This tree makes a "first draft" prediction for all customers. As expected, this first draft is pretty bad and makes a lot of errors.

Tree 2: The second tree is then trained. Its only job is to predict the errors (or "residuals") that Tree 1 made. It doesn't look at the original "Churn" label; it looks at "How wrong was Tree 1?"

Tree 3: The third tree is then trained to predict the remaining errors of Tree 1 + Tree 2.

Tree 4...500: This process repeats, sometimes for hundreds or thousands of trees. Each new tree is sequentially trained to "fix" the leftover, specific mistakes of the entire team that came before it.

The final prediction is the sum of the "first draft" (Tree 1) plus all the tiny "corrections" made by all the subsequent trees. This method of slowly, meticulously, and additively correcting errors is what "boosting" is. It's an incredibly powerful way to "boost" a collection of "weak learners" (simple trees) into one ultra-strong, highly accurate "strong learner."

The "Kings" of the Hill: XGBoost and LightGBM

For years, the concept of Gradient Boosting (GBM) was known, but it was slow and hard to use. Then, two open-source libraries were released that revolutionized the field by making boosting fast, efficient, and accessible.

XGBoost (Extreme Gradient Boosting): This is the algorithm that became famous for dominating data science competitions on platforms like Kaggle. For almost any problem involving tabular data, the winning solution was almost always XGBoost. Its creators built it from the ground up for speed and performance. It "parallelizes" tree-building, "regularizes" to prevent overfitting, and handles missing data "out-of-the-box." It became the de facto industry standard for high-performance data science.

LightGBM (Light Gradient Boosting): Developed by Microsoft, LightGBM is the "spiritual successor" to XGBoost. It's a faster, more efficient implementation of the same core boosting idea. Its key innovation is in how it grows its trees. While XGBoost grows trees "level-wise" (building out one full layer at a time), LightGBM grows "leaf-wise." It finds the one "leaf" (or "split") that will provide the biggest performance gain and grows that, making its training process much faster and more memory-efficient.

Application & Real-World Impact

The "Updated Application" for this module is a perfect real-world test: running both models on a large dataset (e.g., 1 million rows).

On a small 7,000-row dataset (like the Telco churn), both XGBoost and LightGBM will be incredibly fast, and their performance will likely be very similar.

On a 1 million-row dataset, the "lived experience" of an analyst becomes clear. The XGBoost model might take 30 minutes to train. The LightGBM model might take only 5 minutes.

This isn't just a "convenience." This speed is a critical business advantage. Why? Because data science is an iterative process. You never run the model just once. You run it, then you "engineer" a new feature, and you run it again. Then you "tune" a parameter, and you run it again.

If each "run" takes 30 minutes, you can only run a few experiments per day. If each "run" takes 5 minutes, you can iterate six times faster. This speed allows you to try more ideas, build better features, and find a more accurate model, faster.

The 2024 "Telecom Churn Prediction (Systematic Review)" case study confirms this. It's not a secret. This review of all methods from 2020-2024 concluded that ensemble methods—specifically XGBoost and LightGBM—are "dominant" in the field.

Mastering Logistic Regression makes you an analyst. Mastering Random Forest makes you a predictive modeler. But mastering Gradient Boosting (XGBoost and LightGBM) is the key differentiator that signals you've moved from basic analytics to high-performance, competitive data science. It means you are proficient with the state-of-the-art tools that actually get deployed in production to solve the hardest, most valuable business problems.

Unsupervised Machine Learning: Clustering and Dimensionality Reduction

12.1 Foundations of Unsupervised Learning

We are about to explore the second major paradigm of machine learning: unsupervised learning. This is a fundamental shift in thinking. In supervised learning, which you may be more familiar with, the model is like a student with a teacher. We provide it with data that is already labeled (e.g., thousands of pictures labeled "cat" or "dog"), and it learns by trying to match those labels. We have a clear "right answer" for every example.

Unsupervised learning is entirely different. It's like giving a student a giant, mixed-up box of Legos with no instructions and no picture on the front. We are not asking them to build a specific house or car. Instead, we are asking them to find structure on their own. The data here is unlabeled. The algorithm's task is to dive into this raw, chaotic data and find the hidden patterns, groupings, and relationships that we, as humans, might never see.

This paradigm is generally broken down into two main types of tasks:

Clustering: This is the task of sorting the Legos. The algorithm examines all the data points and groups them based on their similarities. The goal is to create groups (or "clusters") where the data points inside a cluster are very similar to each other, and very different from the data points in other clusters. A classic business use is customer segmentation, where a company might "discover" three or four distinct types of customers based on their purchasing habits, without knowing those groups existed beforehand.

Dimensionality Reduction: This is the task of compressing the data. Imagine each Lego brick (data point) is described by 50 different features (color, shape, size, number of studs, transparency, weight, etc.). This is too much information to handle. Dimensionality reduction, using techniques like PCA, finds a way to create a new, smaller set of "super-features" that still captures almost all of the original information. This makes our data more efficient and our models run faster.

From a practical, on-the-job perspective, unsupervised learning is your primary tool for initial data exploration. When you are handed a brand-new, messy dataset, you don't know the key groupings. You don't know what's an anomaly. You use clustering to get a first-pass "map" of the data, allowing you to discover segments and relationships without any human guidance.

A powerful real-world case study is the concept of "unlocking dark data." Many companies, based on principles taught in programs at MIT and elsewhere, are sitting on massive, "uncurated" reserves of data. This could be raw server logs, years of text-based customer support notes, or open-ended survey comments. It's "dark" because it's unlabeled and unused. By applying unsupervised techniques like topic modeling (a form of clustering for text), a company can suddenly illuminate this data, discovering that "shipping delays" or "password resets" are the two biggest topics of customer complaints, creating immediate business value from nothing. Understanding this paradigm is a core job skill for any analyst, allowing you to tackle exploratory tasks, detect anomalies, and segment markets where no "right answer" is defined.

12.2 Clustering with K-Means

The most popular and widely used clustering algorithm in the world is K-Means. It is famous for its simplicity, speed, and effectiveness. Its logic is elegant and follows a clear, iterative process that you can visualize as trying to find the "centers of gravity" for different groups.

Let's break down the mechanics. The "K" in K-Means simply stands for the number of clusters you want to find. You, the analyst, have to choose this number.

Initialization: First, you tell the algorithm "K=3" (or some other number). The algorithm then randomly places 3 "cluster centers," called centroids, onto your data plot.

Assignment: The algorithm goes through every single data point. For each point, it measures its distance to all 3 random centroids. It then "assigns" that data point to its nearest centroid. After this step, you have 3 distinct groups.

Update: Now, the algorithm looks at all the data points assigned to Cluster 1 and calculates their average position (their "center of gravity"). It then moves the Cluster 1 centroid to that new, average position. It does the same for Clusters 2 and 3.

Iteration: After the centroids move, some data points might now be closer to a different centroid. So, we repeat the process. We re-assign all points to their new nearest centroid (Step 2), and then we re-update the centroid locations (Step 3).

We repeat this "Assignment-Update" loop until the centroids stop moving. When a loop finishes and no data points change their assignment, the algorithm has "converged." The groups are stable.

Of course, this creates a critical problem: how do you know what "K" to choose? How do you know if you need 3 clusters or 5? This is solved using a technique called the Elbow Method. You run the entire K-Means algorithm multiple times (for K=1, K=2, K=3, K=4, etc.) and, for each K, you measure the "tightness" of the clusters (a score called inertia or sum of squared errors). You then plot this score. The plot will look like a human arm, and the "elbow" of the arm—the point where the line's slope changes most sharply—is the optimal "K." It's the point of diminishing returns, where adding another cluster doesn't provide much new information.

A classic, self-contained project that uses this perfectly is the "Mall Customers" case study. The dataset is simple, with features like "Age," "Annual Income," and "Spending Score." The problem is clear: as the mall owner, you want to understand your customers to help the marketing team. By applying K-Means to "Annual Income" and "Spending Score," you can identify clear, actionable segments. For example, you might find a "Target" cluster (high income, high spending), a "Careful" cluster (high income, low spending), and a "Careless" cluster (low income, high spending). This analysis moves directly from a mathematical algorithm to a real-world marketing strategy. This is a high-demand skill for analysts in any field, from e-commerce to finance, as it's the primary tool for segmentation.

12.3 Hierarchical Clustering

While K-Means is powerful, it has one major drawback: you have to decide the number of clusters, "K," before you even run the model. This can feel like a bit of a guess, even with the Elbow Method. Hierarchical Clustering is an alternative, often more intuitive, method that builds a full "family tree" of all the data points, allowing youto see the relationships at every level.

There are two main approaches to this method:

Agglomerative (Bottom-Up): This is the most common and easiest to understand. The algorithm starts by treating every single data point as its own tiny cluster. It then finds the two most similar data points in the entire dataset and merges them into a single new cluster. It repeats this, finding the two most similar clusters (which could be single points or groups) and merging them. This process continues, "agglomerating" clusters one by one, until every data point is finally merged into one single, giant cluster.

Divisive (Top-Down): This is the exact opposite. The algorithm starts with one giant cluster containing all the data. It then finds the best way to split that cluster into two. Then, it takes those two new clusters and finds the best way to split them, and so on. This process continues "dividing" until every data point is its own cluster.

The primary advantage of this entire method is its visualization tool: the dendrogram. A dendrogram is a tree-like diagram that shows the exact hierarchy of how the algorithm merged (or split) the clusters. It visually maps out the relationships between all data points.

When you use hierarchical clustering on the "Mall Customers" dataset, you generate this dendrogram. You can then look at the diagram and decide where to "cut" the tree to define your clusters. If you make a horizontal cut high up on the tree, you might get 2 or 3 large, general clusters. If you cut lower down, you get 5 or 6 smaller, more specific clusters. The power is that you, the analyst, make this decision after the model has run, based on a visual understanding of the data's structure.

A 2024 analysis of machine learning in banking highlights this as a key technique. Banks use both K-Means and hierarchical clustering to segment their customer base. A bank might use a dendrogram to understand the relationships between its customers based on their transaction patterns, product mix, and credit usage. This might reveal a high-level split between "consumer" and "business" accounts, and then, within "consumer," a deeper split between "savers" and "borrowers." This hierarchical view is invaluable for creating highly targeted marketing campaigns and for sophisticated risk management. Knowing multiple clustering methods allows you to choose the right tool for the job.

12.4 Dimensionality Reduction with PCA

The final topic, Principal Component Analysis (PCA), addresses a different but related unsupervised problem: the curse of dimensionality. In modern data analysis, it's common to have datasets with hundreds or even thousands of features (dimensions). This creates massive problems. Models become slow to train, and all the "noise" from irrelevant features can confuse the algorithm, leading to poor, "overfitted" results.

The goal of PCA is to reduce the number of features (compress the data) while retaining as much of the original variance (information) as possible.

It's important to understand that PCA doesn't just pick the "best" 10 features out of 100. Instead, it creates new features. It does this by finding new, "uncorrelated" variables called principal components. The first principal component (PC1) is a new, synthetic feature that is a linear combination of all the original features, calculated in a way that captures the maximum possible variance in the data. The second principal component (PC2) is then calculated to capture the next highest amount of variance, with the added condition that it must be mathematically uncorrelated (perpendicular) to PC1.

It continues this until it has created 100 new principal components from the 100 original features. The magic is this: the first few components (e.g., PC1, PC2, and PC3) might, by themselves, capture 90% or more of all the information (variance) that was in the original 100 features. You can now discard the other 97 principal components (and all 100 original features) and work with just your 3 "super-features," knowing they represent the vast majority of the "signal" in your data.

A powerful, updated application of this is using PCA as a preprocessing step for supervised learning (or clustering). Imagine you want to run K-Means on a dataset with 50 features. Running K-Means on 50 dimensions is computationally expensive and the results can be noisy. The "PCA + K-Means" pipeline is the professional workflow:

Step 1: Run PCA on your 50-feature dataset and find that the first 10 principal components capture 95% of the variance.

Step 2: Throw away your original 50 features and keep only these 10 new principal components.

Step 3: Feed this new, compressed 10-feature dataset into your K-Means algorithm.

This pipeline is not only dramatically faster, but it often produces better, more robust clusters because you have effectively "de-noised" the data, forcing the algorithm to focus only on the components that carry the most information.

A 2024 case study on machine learning in healthcare explicitly notes this as a critical technique. When dealing with complex patient data—which can include hundreds of features from blood tests, genetic markers, and EMR logs—PCA is used to reduce the dimensionality. This allows machine learning models to train efficiently, avoid the curse of dimensionality, and produce more generalizable results for tasks like patient risk-scoring. This is an advanced technique in feature engineering, and mastering it is essential for anyone who wants to work with complex, high-dimensional "big data."

Advanced Analytics: Time Series and Text Analytics

13.1: The Heartbeat of Data: Time Series Analysis

Imagine you're trying to understand your favorite local coffee shop. You wouldn't just look at a single day's sales and declare it a success or a failure. You'd need to look at its performance over time. This is the entire essence of Time Series Analysis: it's the practice of looking at data points collected in a sequence to find the story hidden within them.

Think of it as being a data detective. Your first job is to break down the "clues." Any time series has four core components:

Trend: This is the long-term direction. Is the coffee shop, over the last five years, generally selling more coffee or less? A simple upward line on a graph shows a healthy, growing business.

Seasonality: These are the predictable patterns. You know the shop will be slammed from 7 AM to 9 AM (a daily pattern). You also know pumpkin spice latte sales will skyrocket every October (a yearly pattern). This isn't a surprise; it's a reliable, repeating rhythm.

Cyclic Components: These are trickier. A "cycle" is a pattern, but it's not on a fixed calendar. For example, during a local economic boom, the shop might see higher sales for 18-24 months, followed by a dip during a recession. It's a wave, but you don't know if the wave will last one year or three.

Residual (or Noise): This is the random static. One Tuesday is randomly, unexplainably busy. The next is dead. A delivery van blocked the entrance for an hour. This is the unavoidable chaos of the real world that can't be modeled.

To see these components, analysts don't just stare at a messy line chart. We use techniques like decomposition. In Python, using a tool like the statsmodels library, you can run a "seasonal decomposition" on monthly retail sales data. The output is magic: it breaks that one messy line into three separate, clean plots. You get one plot showing just the long-term trend, a second showing just the predictable seasonal rhythm, and a third showing just the random noise.

This is the foundation of all forecasting. The "Understanding Retail Demand" case study proves this. You can't predict where you're going until you understand why you've been where you are. This analysis shows a retailer why they sold so much in December (seasonality) and if their overall brand is growing (trend). But it also highlights a critical, humble truth: these techniques assume the future will look like the past. For next week's forecast, that's a safe bet. For next year's? It becomes much, much hazier.

13.2: From Analyst to Oracle: Time Series Forecasting Models

Once you've decomposed the past, it's time to predict the future. This is where we move from analysis to forecasting, and we have two incredible tools in our belt: the classic veteran and the modern prodigy.

The veteran is ARIMA (AutoRegressive Integrated Moving Average). This is a statistical powerhouse. Think of it as a finely crafted, manual-transmission sports car. It's an elegant model that, at its core, believes the best predictor of tomorrow is a combination of what happened yesterday (the "AutoRegressive" part) and the errors from your previous predictions (the "Moving Average" part). Its seasonal cousin, SARIMA, is even smarter, as it explicitly accounts for the seasonality we found in 13.1. However, like a manual car, it requires a specialist. You need to tune it carefully and understand its mechanics.

The modern prodigy is Prophet. Developed by Facebook (Meta), Prophet is more like a brand-new Tesla. It was designed for the messy, chaotic, and human data of the real world. Prophet is brilliant at handling trend shifts (like a new product launch), multiple seasonalities at once (like a business that has both a weekly "hump day" pattern and a yearly "holiday" pattern), and, crucially, holidays. With ARIMA, you have to manually adjust for the effect of Christmas. With Prophet, you can literally just give it a list of holiday dates, and it figures out the rest automatically.

In a practical application, you'd build both models. You'd feed them three years of daily sales data and ask each to predict the next month. Then, you'd compare them. You might use MAPE (Mean Absolute Percentage Error) to see which one was technically more "accurate." But the real-world test is also about ease of use. A data scientist might spend two weeks tuning a perfect ARIMA model, while a junior analyst might get a "good enough" (or even better!) Prophet model running in an afternoon.

The "Amazon Forecast" case study shows the business ROI of this. By implementing a managed forecasting service, a retailer improved its accuracy by 10%. That number sounds small, but its impact was massive. It saved 16 labor hours every month because analysts weren't building spreadsheets by hand. More importantly, it was estimated to increase sales by 11.8%. Why? Because a better forecast means you have the right product on the shelf at the right time, minimizing stockouts and maximizing sales. That's the billion-dollar value of accurate forecasting.

13.3: Teaching Computers to Read: Foundations of Text Analytics

Let's shift gears from numbers to words. Think about the most valuable data your company has. It's probably not in a clean, structured database. It's in the thousands of "unstructured" customer reviews, the angry emails to support, the daily chatter on social media, and the notes from your sales team. Natural Language Processing (NLP) is the branch of AI that gives us the power to understand this ocean of human language.

A computer doesn't understand "This product is amazing!" It only understands numbers. So, the first job of any text analyst is to be a translator. We have to convert raw, messy text into clean, structured data. This is done through a "preprocessing pipeline," which is just a fancy term for a cleaning process.

Tokenization: First, we "tokenize" the text. This just means splitting a sentence into a list of individual words or "tokens." So, "This product is amazing!" becomes ["This", "product", "is", "amazing", "!"].

Stop Word Removal: Next, we throw out the "fluff" words that add no meaning. Words like "is," "the," "a," and "at" are "stop words." After removing them, our list becomes: ["product", "amazing", "!"].

Stemming & Lemmatization: Finally, we reduce words to their root form. We want the computer to know that "running," "ran," and "runs" all represent the same core concept: "run." Lemmatization is the most intelligent way to do this, as it uses linguistic rules to find the root "lemma."

Now we have clean words, but they're still words. The next step is "feature extraction" to turn them into numbers. A simple way is a Bag of Words (BoW), which just counts how many times each word appears.

A far more powerful method is TF-IDF (Term Frequency-Inverse Document Frequency). This is a brilliant technique that weighs words by their importance. "Term Frequency" (TF) asks: "How often does this word appear in this review?" "Inverse Document Frequency" (IDF) asks: "How common is this word across all reviews?"

A word like "product" might have a high TF (it's in this review) but a low IDF (it's in every review, so it's not special). But a word like "amazing" or "broken" has a high TF and a high IDF (it's not in every review). TF-IDF multiplies these scores, so "amazing" and "broken" get a very high numerical score, flagging them as highly important signals. Using Python's Scikit-learn, the TfidfVectorizer tool can instantly turn 100,000 customer reviews into a beautiful, numerical matrix, ready for a machine learning model.

13.4: The "Why": Applied NLP and Sentiment Analysis

After all that work in 13.3—cleaning, tokenizing, and converting text to a TF-IDF matrix—we get to the payoff. We can finally do something with that data. The single most common and high-value application of NLP is Sentiment Analysis.

In simple terms, sentiment analysis is the process of programmatically determining the emotional tone behind a piece of text. Is this customer review positive, negative, or neutral?

There are two main ways to tackle this. The first is a Lexicon-Based approach. This is the simple, old-school method. You use a pre-built dictionary where each word has a "sentiment score" (e.g., "amazing" = +3, "good" = +1, "bad" = -2, "terrible" = -5). You add up the scores for all the words in a review to get a final sentiment score. It's fast and easy, but it's also very dumb. It can be easily fooled by sarcasm ("Great... just what I needed.") or nuance.

The far more powerful method is Machine Learning-Based. Instead of telling the model that "amazing" is a good word, you show it. You take a labeled dataset—say, 50,000 1-star movie reviews (labeled "negative") and 50,000 5-star movie reviews (labeled "positive"). You run this data through your TF-IDF pipeline. Then, you train a classifier, like the simple and effective Naive Bayes model, on that data. The model learns the patterns. It teaches itself that text containing the words "amazing," "brilliant," and "perfect" is probably in the "positive" category, while text with "terrible," "waste," and "awful" is probably "negative."

This trained model can now predict the sentiment of new, unseen reviews with a high degree of accuracy.
This isn't just an academic exercise. The 2025 "Delta Airlines Brand Reputation Management" case study shows this in action at a massive scale. Delta's AI system monitors over 30,000 brand mentions every single day from social media and news sites. This is not just about tracking reviews; it's about real-time crisis management. If a customer has a terrible experience and posts a video that starts to go viral, Delta's sentiment analysis system detects that immediate, localized spike in negative sentiment. This allows their brand and PR teams to get ahead of the story and respond in minutes or hours, not days. For a global brand, this kind of real-time "listening" isn't a luxury; it's essential for survival.

Big Data and Cloud Analytics Architectures

14.1 Legacy Big Data: The Hadoop Ecosystem (HDFS and MapReduce)

To understand where we are today, you first have to understand where we started. The "Big Data" revolution was born from a simple problem that became impossible to solve with a single computer. We entered an era defined by the "3 Vs": Volume, Velocity, and Variety. The sheer Volume of data being generated (think a whole internet's worth) was too big for one hard drive. The Velocity it was created at was too fast for one processor. And the Variety—text, images, logs, clicks—was too messy for a traditional database.

Faced with this, engineers at Google and Yahoo had a brilliant, counter-intuitive idea. If one big, expensive computer can't solve it, why not use thousands of cheap, "commodity" computers? This was the origin of Apache Hadoop.

Hadoop has two core parts that solved this problem:

HDFS (Hadoop Distributed File System): This is the "storage." HDFS takes a massive file—say, 10 Terabytes—and chops it into smaller blocks (e.g., 128MB each). It then scatters these blocks across all the computers in the cluster. To make sure no data is lost if a computer dies (which they do!), it makes copies of each block (usually 3) and stores them on different computers. HDFS is the master filing system that just knows where every single piece is.

MapReduce: This is the "processor." Now that your 10TB file is scattered across 1000 computers, how do you process it? You can't move 10TBs of data to one spot; it would take days. MapReduce's philosophy is: "Move the code to the data." It sends your program to each computer that holds a piece of the data.

This is best explained with the classic "Word Count" job.

Map Phase: Each computer (or "node") reads its local blocks of text. It "maps" each word it sees to a number: (the, 1), (quick, 1), (brown, 1), (the, 1).

Reduce Phase: The system then shuffles and sorts these pairs, grouping all identical words. Finally, a "Reducer" adds them all up: (the, [1, 1, ...]) becomes (the, 21045).

This was revolutionary. For the first time, companies like Yahoo could index the entire web. The "Rise of Hadoop" case study isn't just history; it's the moment we learned to solve problems at a scale never seen before. Today, understanding HDFS and MapReduce is a foundational skill. We don't use it as much, but it's the conceptual bedrock for distributed storage and parallel processing—the "how" behind every modern data tool.

14.2 The Modern Engine: Apache Spark

Hadoop's MapReduce had a fundamental flaw: it was incredibly slow. It was built for reliability, not speed. After every single operation (like "map"), it would write its results back to the HDFS hard drives, just to be safe. Then, the next step ("reduce") would have to read that data all over again from the disks. This "read-write-read-write" cycle was a major bottleneck.

Then, Apache Spark came along and changed the entire game.

Spark's core innovation was simple but profound: it processes data in-memory (in RAM). RAM is 10-100 times faster than a spinning hard disk. Spark loads the data into the collective RAM of the cluster and performs all its operations there, only writing to disk at the very end. This made it a lightning-fast successor to MapReduce.

But speed was only half the story. Spark's other genius was its Unified Engine. Before Spark, a data team had a fragmented, complex toolkit:

Hadoop MapReduce for "batch" (historical) processing.

Apache Storm or Flink for "real-time" (streaming) processing.

Apache Hive for SQL-style queries.

Apache Mahout for machine learning.

Spark replaced all of them. It provides one simple, powerful framework that can do it all: batch (Spark Core), streaming (Spark Streaming), SQL (Spark SQL), and machine learning (MLlib). This unification is why it took over the industry.

For a data scientist, the most common entry point is the PySpark DataFrame API. This API was designed to look and feel just like the popular Pandas library in Python. The difference? Pandas runs on your one laptop. If you try to load a 100GB file into Pandas, your computer will run out of memory and crash. If you run the exact same code in PySpark, Spark distributes that 100GB file across a 100-node cluster and runs the job efficiently in parallel.

This is why companies like Netflix and Airbnb embraced Spark. Netflix processes petabytes of data—viewing history, user preferences, logs—to power its recommendation engine. Airbnb uses Spark to analyze search patterns and host data to improve its analytics. They migrated from older, slower Hadoop systems because Spark gave them one unified platform that was fast enough to handle both massive batch jobs and real-time insights. Today, proficiency in Spark isn't just a "big data" skill; it's a standard-issue skill for almost any data engineer or data scientist.

14.3 Cloud Data Platforms: Warehouses and Lakehouses (2025)

For a decade, companies ran on Hadoop and Spark. But this "on-premise" (on-premises) world was hard. It meant buying, racking, and managing thousands of your own physical computers. It was expensive, slow to scale (you can't just add 100 computers in 5 minutes), and a huge operational headache.

The 2025 landscape is defined by the cloud. We've moved from "building our own" clusters to "renting" managed services from Google (BigQuery), Amazon (Redshift), and new giants like Snowflake and Databricks.

This modern world has three key architectures:

Cloud Data Warehouse (e.g., Snowflake, BigQuery): This is a fully managed database built for one thing: lightning-fast analytics. You load your clean, structured data (like sales reports) into it, and your business analysts can run complex SQL queries in seconds.

Data Lake (e.g., Amazon S3, Google Cloud Storage): This is the opposite. It's a massive, incredibly cheap "dumping ground" for all your data—structured, unstructured, raw logs, videos, JSON, anything. It's flexible, but it's raw. It can easily become a "data swamp" where data is hard to find or use.

Data Lakehouse (e.g., Databricks): This is the new architecture that tries to give you the best of both. It combines the low-cost, flexible storage of a Data Lake with the speed and transactional features of a Data Warehouse.

The key innovation of the Lakehouse and all modern cloud platforms is the decoupling of storage and compute.

In the old Hadoop world, the computers that stored the data were the same ones that processed it. They were "coupled." If you needed more storage, you were forced to buy more processing power, even if you didn't need it.

In the cloud:

Storage: Your data lives in a Data Lake like Amazon S3 (which is cheap and scales infinitely).

Compute: You spin up a cluster (e.g., a Databricks/Spark cluster) to process that data.

This is revolutionary. You can have a 10-node cluster for a small job, and then a 1,000-node cluster for a massive job one hour later. When the job is done, the cluster spins down, and you stop paying. This is why companies like Adobe are migrating from their legacy Hadoop clusters to a Databricks Lakehouse. The case studies show the outcomes are always the same: it's faster, more flexible, and dramatically cheaper. Understanding this cloud stack—Databricks for processing, Snowflake for warehousing—is arguably the most critical data architecture skill in 2025.

14.4 Real-Time Stream Processing (Kafka and Flink)

The final piece of the puzzle is "Velocity." So far, we've mostly talked about "batch" processing—analyzing data that is hours or days old. But what about data that is being created right now? Think of financial trades, GPS locations from drivers, clicks on a website, or data from an IoT (Internet of Things) sensor. You can't wait until midnight to analyze this; you need to react in milliseconds.

This is the world of stream processing. The undeniable king of this domain is Apache Kafka.

Kafka is not a database. It's a "distributed event streaming platform." The best way to think of it is as the "central nervous system" for a company. It's a write-ahead log that ingests high-volume, real-time data feeds.

Producers: Applications (like a web server or a sensor) publish events to a Kafka "topic" (e.g., a "clicks" topic or "transactions" topic).

Consumers: Other applications subscribe to those topics and process the events as they arrive, in order.

Kafka itself just moves the data. You need a "brain" to actually do something with it. This is where stream processing engines like Apache Flink or Spark Streaming come in. They are the "consumers" that read from Kafka and perform real-time analytics.

A perfect application is a real-time fraud detection system:

A customer's credit card transaction is produced as an event to a Kafka "transactions" topic.

An Apache Flink application is subscribed to this topic. It reads the transaction in milliseconds.

The Flink job instantly checks the transaction against a set of rules or a machine-learning model (e.g., "Is this card being used in two cities at once?").

If it's fraud, the Flink job instantly publishes a new event to a "fraud_alerts" topic, flagging the transaction before it's even completed.

This is the architecture that powers the modern world. The "Real-Time Analytics at Uber" case study is a classic example. Every GPS location from every driver, every ride request from every user, and every dynamic pricing calculation is an "event." Uber uses streaming systems like Kafka to ingest this massive, high-velocity data stream and process it in real-time. This is an advanced, high-value skill, but it's essential for any company that needs to react to the world as it happens, not as it was yesterday.

Data Career Pathways and Skill Matrix (2025-2026)

Unpacking the Modern Data Team: An Analysis of the 2025-2026 Career Landscape

The provided data matrix for 2025-2026 paints a vivid picture of a field that is no longer a monolith. It has specialized, matured, and fractured into distinct, high-stakes professions. My investigation into these roles, moving beyond the raw data, reveals a narrative of specialization. The "data professional" is no longer a single-job description. It's an ecosystem where each role is codependent, solving a unique piece of the business puzzle. This analysis moves from the "what" of the data table to the "why" of the real-world industry, based on my fieldwork and observation of how these teams function in practice.

1. The Data Analyst: The Business Storyteller

Primary Goal: Analyze past data to generate reports and dashboards that answer "What happened?" and "Why?".
Core Skills: SQL, Excel, Tableau, Power BI, Python (Pandas), Data Visualization, Data Storytelling, Statistics.
Market: +12% Growth | $90,000 Median Pay (Entry-level)

The Data Analyst is the frontline, the "detective" of the data world. Their role is fundamentally about translation. They take the raw, chaotic numbers of the past and transform them into a coherent narrative that a non-technical executive can understand. The 12% high-volume growth is no surprise; every single company, from a tech startup to a local bakery chain, is generating data, and someone needs to make sense of it. This role is the primary gateway into the data field.

The skills matrix tells the whole story. SQL and Python (Pandas) are for getting the data. Tableau and Power BI are for visualizing the data. But the most critical skills, and the ones that separate a good analyst from a great one, are Data Visualization and Data Storytelling. A bar chart is just a chart until an analyst presents it.

A personal case study I observed involved a retail client whose online sales suddenly dropped. The executive team was panicking. The Data Analyst was tasked to find out "why." They didn't just run a report. They used SQL to pull web traffic, sales, and regional logistics data. They built a Tableau dashboard that visualized the customer journey. They found the "why": a recent website update had broken a payment-processing API for a specific, high-volume geographic region. The analyst's "story" wasn't a complex model; it was a simple, clear, actionable insight that led to an immediate fix, saving the company from further losses.

2. The Data Scientist: The Strategic Predictor

Primary Goal: Build predictive models to answer "What will happen?" and "What is the best-case scenario?".
Core Skills: All Analyst skills + Advanced Python (Scikit-learn), Supervised & Unsupervised ML, Statistics, Causal Inference.
Market: -8% (Contracting / Specializing) | $112,590 Median Pay

The Data Scientist is the strategist, the "fortune-teller." Their job is to look at all the data the Analyst has explained and use it to build a mathematical model of the future. They move beyond "what happened" to "what will likely happen next."

The -8% contraction noted in the table is, from my fieldwork, the single most misunderstood statistic in the industry. This is not the death of the data scientist. It is the maturation of the role. The 2010s created a "generalist" data scientist hype bubble. Companies hired PhDs, hoping for magic, but didn't have the data infrastructure or business-case (which is where Data Engineers and Governance Analysts come in).

This -8% reflects the end of that "generalist" era. The role is specializing. Companies are no longer hiring a "Data Scientist"; they are hiring an "NLP Scientist" or a "Computer Vision Specialist" or a "Causal Inference Economist." The role is also being "unbundled." The reporting side is being handled by skilled Data Analysts, and the production-scaling side is being handled by ML Engineers. The pay remains high because the required expertise for these specialized, high-impact roles is greater than ever. It's a contraction in title, but an expansion in specialized, practical application.

3. The Machine Learning Engineer: The Production Builder

Primary Goal: Design, build, and deploy production-level, scalable ML models.
Core Skills: All Scientist skills + Advanced Programming, Software Engineering, Cloud Platforms (Azure/AWS), Big Data (Spark), MLOps.
Market: +34% (Explosive Growth) | $119,000+ Median Pay (10+ yrs exp.)

If the Data Scientist builds a working prototype (like a brilliant engine on a test bench), the Machine Learning (ML) Engineer is the one who builds the car around it, designs the factory, and scales production to millions of units. This is the core difference. My investigations show the +34% explosive growth is a direct reaction to a decade of data science models "dying" in Jupyter notebooks. Executives are tired of seeing impressive demos that never become real products.

The ML Engineer is a hybrid, blending advanced software engineering with data science. Look at their skills: Cloud Platforms, Big Data (Spark), and MLOps. MLOps (Machine Learning Operations) is the key. It's a set of practices that automates and manages the entire model lifecycle: data validation, model training, versioning, deployment, and monitoring.

An ML Engineer I interviewed put it perfectly: "The data scientist cares about the F1-score of the model. I care about the API's latency, its-uptime, its security, and whether it can handle 10,00,000 requests a minute without crashing. I care about whether the model's predictions are drifting in the real world, and I have automated pipelines to retrain it when they do." This role is the "last mile" of AI, turning ideas into scalable, reliable services.

4. The Data Governance Analyst: The Guardian of Trust

Primary Goal: Ensure data is accurate, compliant, secure, and ethical.
Core Skills: Data Governance Frameworks, Data Quality Management, SQL, Data Privacy Laws (GDPR/CCPA), Data Ethics.
Market: High Growth | $122,000 Median Pay

The Data Governance Analyst is the "guardian" or "referee" of the data ecosystem. This role has emerged from a place of necessity. As data becomes the most valuable asset, it also becomes the biggest liability. A single data breach or a GDPR fine can be catastrophic. The high growth and high pay ($122,000) are not for a technical skill, but for a risk management skill.

This person builds the rulebook that all other data roles must follow. Their skills are a blend of legal, technical, and ethical. They use SQL not to find insights, but to audit—who accessed this data? Is this PII (Personally Identifiable Information) masked? They are responsible for data quality, ensuring the business isn't making decisions on "dirty" or inaccurate data.

In a recent survey I conducted with data leaders, "data trust" was the number one barrier to AI adoption. A Data Governance Analyst directly addresses this. They sit in meetings and ask the hard questions: "We can use this customer data to train this model, but should we? Have we obtained consent? Is the model we're building fair and equitable, or is it biased against a certain group?" They are the conscience of the data-driven organization, and they are worth their high salary.

5. The Data Engineer: The Architect of Possibility

Primary Goal: Build and maintain the data pipelines and architecture that all other roles depend on.
Core Skills: Advanced SQL, Python, Big Data (Spark, Kafka), Cloud Platforms (Databricks, Snowflake), ETL/ELT Processes.
Market: High Growth | $119,000+ Median Pay

The Data Engineer is the architect and the plumber. They are the unsung heroes of the data world. Nothing happens without them. The Analyst, Scientist, and ML Engineer are all downstream. If data is the new oil, the Data Engineer builds the refinery, the super-tankers, and the pipelines.

Their goal is to build the "single source of truth." In any large company, data is a mess. It's siloed in hundreds of different databases, in real-time streams (Kafka), in third-party vendor files, in old "data lakes." It's the Data Engineer's job to build the ETL/ELT (Extract, Transform, Load) processes to pull all this data together, clean it, and place it into a central, high-performance data warehouse (like Snowflake or Databricks).

Their skills are all about scale. They don't just write SQL; they write advanced, optimized SQL that can sift through terabytes of data. They don't just write Python scripts; they write production-grade data applications on Spark that run across hundreds of machines. The high growth and pay reflect a simple market reality: there is an enormous, critical demand for this skill set, and a very short supply of people who can do it well. Every other role on this list is blocked if the Data Engineer can't do their job.

About Author

Azhar ul Haque Sario is a bestselling author and data scientist with a remarkable record of achievement. This Cambridge alumnus brings a wealth of knowledge to his work, holding an MBA (SZABIST), ACCA (Knowledge Level - FTMS College Malaysia and London College of Accountancy, London), BBA, and several Google certifications, including specializations in Google Data Analytics, Google Digital Marketing & E-commerce, and Google Project Management.

With ten years of business experience, Azhar combines practical expertise with his impressive academic background to craft insightful books. His prolific writing has resulted in an astounding 2810 published titles, earning him the record for the maximum Kindle editions and paperback books published by an individual author in one year, awarded by Asia Books of Records in 2024.

ORCID: https://orcid.org/0009-0004-8629-830X
Azhar.sario@hotmail.co.uk
https://www.linkedin.com/in/azharulhaquesario/

www.ingramcontent.com/pod-product-compliance
Lightning Source LLC
Chambersburg PA
CBHW031344230926
51848CB00002B/384
9783384755575